For Review in:

Contemporary Sociology
University of Connecticut
Storrs, CT 06268

400 words
Date 11/30/82

ENVIRONMENTAL DECISION MAKING IN RURAL LOCALES

ENVIRONMENTAL DECISION MAKING IN RURAL LOCALES

The Pine Barrens

Joan Goldstein

PRAEGER

PRAEGER SPECIAL STUDIES • PRAEGER SCIENTIFIC

Library of Congress Cataloging in Publication Data

Goldstein, Joan.
　Environmental decision making in rural locales.

　Bibliography: p.
　1. Land use, Rural—New Jersey—Pine Barrens—Planning. 2. Environmental protection—New Jersey—Pine Barrens. 3. Pine Barrens (N.J.)—Economic conditions. I. Title.
HD266.N5G64		333.76′17′097493		81-5208
ISBN 0-03-059604-1					AACR2

Published in 1981 by Praeger Publishers
CBS Educational and Professional Publishing
A Division of CBS, Inc.
521 Fifth Avenue, New York, New York 10175 U.S.A.

© 1981 by Praeger Publishers

All rights reserved

123456789　145　987654321

Printed in the United States of America

FOREWORD
Denton E. Morrison

Those who favor "use" and who want to characterize land use conflicts as "use versus preservation" oversimplify and bias their case. There is the implication in such language that no utilization, or at best some trivial use, of the resource is what their adversaries have in mind.

This study of the Pine Barrens shows that in a concrete case things are much more complex. The study makes it clear that the Pine Barrens has its traditional uses and users. The conflict is much more rural versus urban use, agricultural versus industrial use, traditional versus modern use than one of simply preserving a natural area against any use at all. At least in the present case, and doubtless in many others, the term "use" in the "preservation versus use" characterization refers to the values of those who want to change the use. Those resisting such change are, however, far from being a homogeneous environmental elite. Nor are all those favoring change predatory capitalists.

The Pine Barrens is a natural area and rural setting in southern New Jersey. It has been the subject of intense political and social conflicts between conservation and development interest groups. The sound of this conflict has been reported on the front pages of the New York Times, the Philadelphia Inquirer, and the Wall Street Journal.

Dr. Goldstein's study on natural resources and land use control in the Pine Barrens is a most significant contribution to the environmental studies literature. This book successfully deals with the history of settlement and population pressure, with changing definitions of resource values, and with the complexities of institutional politics at governmental levels. There are only a small handful of comparable studies at this level of quality.

The book deals with people as well as politics. It is an historical and ethnographic analysis of the social forces that shape public policy, environmental decisions, and land use planning for the rural parts of metropolitan regions. The message of the study is much broader, however.

The land uses at conflict in the Pine Barrens are the more or less traditional ones of agricultural use versus housing, commercial, transportation, and recreational development, but the case is a microcosm of the larger forces and processes that are involved in new conflicts over, for example, strip mining, toxic waste disposal (including radiological wastes), and synfuel development. There are, of course, differences between intraregional cases such as the Pine Barrens and the developing interregional conflicts, but an all too common feature is the displacement of costs and risks to rural areas, while the main benefits go to urban settings.

The broad issues of this study and the processes of conflict it reveals have an importance in enlightening our understanding that goes beyond the particular, although intrinsically interesting and important, case of the Pine Barrens. The study is also an exemplar of how careful and qualitative case studies provide this understanding.

It will provide small comfort for those who want to see environmental conflict issues defined as use versus preservation, but for all who are concerned with genuinely understanding land use conflicts in the context of environmental as well as other concerns it will be of great interest.

ACKNOWLEDGMENTS

This study was funded in part by a research fellowship from The Resources for the Future Foundation, Inc.

There were many who contributed to the completion of this study. To begin with, I am deeply indebted to William Kornblum of the Graduate Center at City University of New York for pointing my interests toward this exhaustive study of the Pine Barrens. His enthusiasm was based on our earlier collaborations on research for the National Park Service, and Dr. Kornblum encouraged my successful application for the fellowship from the Resources for the Future Foundation.

I am indebted to a number of other sociologists as well: to Irving Louis Horowitz for his insights and suggestions on publishing this study; to Suzanne Keller and David Caplovitz for their consistent support of the merit of this work. Bogdan Denitch, Sylvia Fava, Joseph Bensman, and Rolf Meyersohn reviewed the manuscript and offered their thoughts, as did Harold Proshansky, president of the Graduate Center.

From the government of the State of New Jersey, I was offered cooperation, assistance, and even encouragement toward the completion of this study. In particular, I wish to thank Congressman James J. Florio and Governor Brendan Byrne, who offered their time and ideas for interviews, and a corps of congressmen and -women, assemblymen and -women, and state commissioners, many of whom shared their time and expertise.

I cannot begin to thank the people of the Pine Barrens for their assistance, time, cooperation, and generous hospitality during the several years of my field work and ongoing study. I particularly appreciate the hospitality of the Pine Coners—Sam Hunt, Gladys Eayre, Janice Brittin, Uncle Bill Brittin, and Joe Albert—who provided hours of taped interviews. In addition, there was the help and hospitality of Mayor Floyd West and his family, Bill Haines and his family, Charles Thompson Jr. and his family, and particularly, Mary Ann Thompson.

Finally, I wish to thank Ethel Goldstein, my mother, who not only believed in my work but generously offered to type this manuscript.

CONTENTS

	Page
FOREWORD by Denton E. Morrison	v
ACKNOWLEDGMENTS	vii
LIST OF TABLES	xii
LIST OF MAPS	xiii
INTRODUCTION	1
Basis of the Study	2
Historical Roots: The American Concern with the Environment	4
Social Class and Social Policy	7
Preservationists and Conservationists	8
Agricultural Populism and the Rugged Individualist	9
Growth and Containment	9
Relevant Aspects of Land Use Theory	10
Background and Hypothesis	13
Finding and Assessing Information	15

PART I: POPULATION AND THE HUMAN ECOLOGY OF THE PINE BARRENS

INTRODUCTION TO PART I	20
1 EARLY SETTLEMENTS AND TECHNOLOGICAL CHANGE	21
Boundaries	22
Early History	26
Indians	26
Quakers	27
The Iron Forge Industry	29
Impact of Industrial Decline	31
Population	31
Summary	36

Chapter		Page
2	HUMAN SETTLEMENTS: PEOPLE OF THE PINES	37
	The Pineys: Isolation and Poverty	39
	Fielding for Cultural Bias	40
	The Social Significance of Social Darwinism	43
	The Social Consequences for Pineys	44
	Social Class and Moral Codes: The Piney Is Different	45
	Pineys as Nonparticipants in the Planning Drama	49
	Farmers and Small Businessmen: Politics and Public Participation	50
	The Farming Community and the Politics of Land Use	50
	The Decline of Agriculture on a Small Scale	52
	The Newcomers: Retirement Villages and Suburban Development	53
3	THE PINE BARRENS IN THE 1960S: CONFLICTS BETWEEN CONSERVATION AND DEVELOPMENT POLICIES	55
	Suburban Development and Agricultural Decline	56
	The Pine Barrens Awakes to Urban Pressures	57
	The Jetport Controversy	58
	The Plan for the Jetport: The Port of New York Authority	59
	Primary Jetport Site: The Great Swamp	61
	Final Choice for the Jetport Site: Enter the Pine Barrens	63
	The Politics of Land Use and the Race for Governor	64
	Environmental Conflicts and Economic Expansion	66
	The Jetport and Rural Settlements in the Pine Barrens	68
	Economic Incentives	69
	Interest-Group Formation: Opposition to the Jetport	71
	The Military as an Interest Group	73
	The Race for Governor and Pinelands Politics: 1969-70	75
	Summary	79
4	WATER AND LAND: CRANBERRIES AND HOUSING	81
	The Union of Land and Water: Cranberry Growing	81
	Conflict: Monopolizing a Valuable Resource	85

Chapter	Page
Urban Decentralization in the Pine Barrens: Housing and Land	89
Social Change: Retirement Villages as Rural Suburbia	91
Housing and New Towns in the Pines	92
Bass River Township: A Community without Change	93
Pluralism in the 1970s	95

PART II: THE ELABORATION OF INTERESTS—FROM PROTEST TO FORMAL ORGANIZATION

	Page
INTRODUCTION TO PART II	98

5 CLEAVAGE AND ORGANIZATIONAL STRATEGY — 99

Planning as a Rational System of Control	100
Systems of Local Control in Formalized Interest Groups: The Property Owners' Strategy	101
Strategies of the PEC: Power and Local Control	104
Policy Advisory Groups	108
The Environmentalists: State and Federal Strategy	109
Unexpected Allies	112
Cleavage of Environmental Interest Groups	112
Analysis of Political Alignments	114
Local Control versus Federal Control	116

6 EMERGING INSTITUTIONAL ARRANGEMENTS FOR LAND USE POLICIES — 118

Farmland Assessment Act	119
The Control of Water: State Arrangements for Land Use	121
Federal Participation	125
What the Florio Bill Authorized	126
The Governor's Pinelands Review Committee: 1977	127
The Harrison Williams Solution: The Pinelands Planning Commission, 1979	128
The Pine Barrens in the 1980s: Intervention and Crisis	129
Summary	134

7 THE LAND ETHIC AND SOCIAL CHANGE — 137

How Social Change Impacts upon the Pine Barrens	138

	Page
Findings	139
A Historical Perspective	141
Modern Environmental Conflicts	142
Megalopolis as a Social Setting	142
The Decline of the Agricultural Society in an Industrial Society	143
Change and Then Conflict: The Recent Past	144
Theoretical Perspectives	146
Citizens Join the Bureaucracy: The New Era of Land Planning Commissions	147
Comparisons with Canadian Environmental Decision Making	148
New Systems of Government Stewardship	151
Conclusions: The Great Land Transformation	152
APPENDIX	154
Community Study on a Regional Scale	154
Selection of a Region for Study	154
Description of the Pine Barrens	155
Choice of Method: Participant Observation, Historical Analysis, and Quantitative Data	155
BIBLIOGRAPHY	159
ABOUT THE AUTHOR	170

LIST OF TABLES

Table		Page
1	Iron Forge Communities in the New Jersey Pine Barrens	32
2	Change in Pine Barrens Population, 1900-05	34
3	Change in Pine Barrens Population from Civil War to Turn of Century	35
4	Land Use Policies Drafted during Election Years, 1960-77	78
5	Percent of Open Land (Farmland and Woodland) in Ocean County over Two Decades	90
6	Percent of Open Land (Farmland and Woodland) in Burlington County over Two Decades	90
7	Interest-Group Formation in the Pine Barrens	113

LIST OF MAPS

Map		Page
1	The Pine Barrens and the Northeast	25
2	Pine Barrens Area Covered by Proposed Water Quality Standards	122
3	Pine Barrens Protection and Preservation Areas Designated by the Pinelands Review Committee	136

ENVIRONMENTAL
DECISION MAKING
IN RURAL LOCALES

INTRODUCTION

> The highway shrank to two lanes and we were in the
> country. The change was not gradual; you could
> have stopped the car and got out at the exact point
> where suburbia ended and the red-neck South began.
> Dickey, 1970:37

In striking contrast to the oil refineries, clusters of petrochemical plants, and eight-lane superhighways crammed with commuters that most people have come to identify with New Jersey, the Pine Barrens in the southernmost third of the state is an enigma: It is an urban wilderness of some million acres of woodland and farmland, pine forests, remote places called "Hog Wallow" and "Apple Pie Hill," folk legends that conjure up a recalcitrant "Jersey Devil," and the accompanying flavor of rural life styles.

When local residents, environmentalists, academics, legislators, bureaucrats, and recreationists speak nostalgically about New Jersey's Pine Barrens, their vanishing wilderness, they note the presence of rare plant and animal species such as tree frogs and pine snakes, extensive systems of surface water, canoes paddling along narrow and winding rivers, and the almost legendary underground river, the aquifer.

In winter, the frozen cranberry bogs glisten in the pale sunlight of an arctic north. The wind in the flat, open plains cuts sharply across whatever skin dares show through the layers of wool sweaters, hats, mufflers, and assorted protectors from the frigid landscape.

In spring and fall, but most particularly in summer, the region becomes almost tropical. The woods are thick with pungent cedar stands, or strangely stunted "dwarf" pine trees, spindly bushes no more than four feet in height. Trees, the lone inhabitants of the dwarf pine forest, present an undisturbed view for miles of open space and the broad expanse of sky.

Along the narrow and winding rivers, a canoe can move sinuously through tributaries no wider than the width of the canoe. Low, overhanging branches tangle the hair and catch the threads of a shirt; and from time to time the twisted mounds of branches near the shore remind us that there are beavers at work, though there is not a glimpse of them. Driving along the two-lane black-topped unmarked roads, there are rarely signs of houses, or of people who might live in them.

It is precisely this setting, the rural region couched within the highly urban locale, that provides the stage, the drama, and the players of an intense social and political conflict over the land, the water, and the resource management policies.

BASIS OF THE STUDY

This study is a historic and ethnographic analysis of the social forces that shape the planning of a natural area in an urban region. That region, the Pine Barrens in southern New Jersey, is the largest undeveloped portion of land on the eastern seaboard, a national resource that has received attention from the international scientific community, a unique ecosystem within easy commuting distance from the most densely populated urban agglomeration in the nation.

After centuries of rural isolation, abruptly—within the 20 years between the early 1960s and 1980—the region, marked by a variety of extraordinary features with respect to biology, geology, hydrology, and history, has been the focus of social and political conflicts over the use of both the land and the water. The theme that characterizes this conflict—land (and water) as a commodity versus land as a resource—may prove to be the unintended consequence of an industrial and technological advance that has laid claims to the last remaining portions of open space within the United States and, more particularly, on the Eastern seaboard; but the furnace in which these issues are forged is well within the framework of social and environmental planning. Therefore, a general aim of the research was to develop a "natural history" of planning for the preservation and use of large tracts of underdeveloped land close to centers of dense population. Since the history of social environmental planning is a history of political conflicts among factions, interest groups, and governmental institutions, all of whom seek to speak in the name of society, the specific aim of this research was to identify specific interest-group formations and networks that interconnect with large-scale institutional structures in the society. These institutions in turn influence not only the outcome of environmental public policy but also the definition of the problems to begin with.

Alaska, for example, has been the center of heated debate over the Department of the Interior's plan to protect 92 million acres of federal lands by designating them as national parks, wildlife refuges, scenic rivers, and wilderness areas. Supporting an alternative preservation policy through legislation introduced by Representative Morris Udall are 80 cosponsoring congressmen and a coalition of citizen and conservation groups. This mix of preservation interest groups includes federal agencies, legislators, and organized citizen interest groups who define the problem as a preservation versus development exploitation issue. Those opposed to the legislation—representatives of mining, timber, and hunting industries—cite this recent wilderness preservation move as a federal "land grab." Each faction defines the other as exploiter of the land.

Policy decisions are forged through the compilation of the interests of industrial and business enterprise and the proponents of social planning by government regulation. Interest groups emerge around environmental issues, creating an even further division in pluralism, and interconnect with voluntary organizations, such as the Sierra Club, or opposing trade-business organizations, such as mining associations. These subdividing interest groups create pressure for the mobilization of power toward the growth or containment of government activity on natural resource management and planning.

The legitimacy of government resource management is based on the premise that private enterprise and the market economy entail only the short-term exploitation of an ecologically vulnerable resource. Nash (1973:x), for example, makes the point that

> natural resource policy, for example, is one of the best places to examine the tension between individual freedom and social purpose. Enlightened use of the land demands a limitation on the action of a landowner because the easiest, or most lucrative, method of exploiting a resource is seldom in the best long-term interests of the nation as a whole.

Examining the tension between individual freedom and social purpose with respect to environmental decision making requires the in-depth analysis of interest-group formation and networks that interconnect with powerful structures in the society. It is these social forces that aid or impede the public policy formation with respect to land use. Therefore, as an alternative to basing its assumptions on prescriptive deals for natural land and preservation, this research takes one actual case of land use planning and attempts to discover in it the issue definitions and interest-group formations that either aid or impede the ultimate enactment of particular land use policies.

Thus this study is not designed to test a theory of methodology of land use planning, such as one finds in the writing of Ebenezer Howard or Ian McHarg. Instead, we have selected an empirical case of natural area planning and seek to discover principles that apply in possible future projects. Moreover, what is examined is the impact of a social movement on the formation of social policy. The environmental decision-making process has been defined as a social movement that has generated some influence on land use policies (Sills 1975; Morrison et al. 1972). The social forces in the environmental movement affect not only decisions and outcomes but also the process of issue definition as well. Thus Morrison et al. (1972:277) conclude in their study of the environmental movement that "[the] movement is, itself, a significant force in affecting the way environmental problems are defined and addressed."

HISTORICAL ROOTS: THE AMERICAN CONCERN WITH THE ENVIRONMENT

The american concern with the environment began with the wilderness preservation movement in or before the mid-1850s. The spokesmen—John James Audubon, James Fenimore Cooper, Thomas Cole, Francis Parkman, and John Muir—were philosophical leaders whose ideology focused on the preservation of the wilderness for spiritual and esthetic values.

Romanticism in Europe and later in the United States was a revolt against the narrowness of the age of reason: The human soul could not be reduced to a thinking machine. There were certain spiritual and esthetic values that could be developed in appreciation of the marvels of nature, the belief of democracy, and the insistence upon freedom as opposed to authority (Foerster 1947). These beliefs could find their inspiration within the vastness of Western lands, the frontier where individuality and optimism could flourish close to nature and to the natural "goodness" of the human soul.

Within that American romantic movement emerged a movement known as Transcendentalism, which was simultaneously a philosophic, social, and literary movement, highly idealistic, mystical, and individualistic and based upon broad fundamental intuitive truths that transcended human experience. Transcendentalists, Henry David Thoreau, for example, wrote that the natural world symbolized or reflected spiritual truth and moral law. "Instead of calling on some scholar, I paid many a visit to particular trees," wrote Thoreau of his wilderness retreat to Walden Pond (Thoreau 1927:181).

Spiritual truth and "natural law" are found in the character structure of James Fenimore Cooper's Natty Bumppo in The Leather Stocking Tales. Bumppo is a noble scout who lives in the woodlands, like the Indians, and, as a result of his harmony with nature, stands as a protest on behalf of simplicity and perfect freedom against encroaching law and order (Cooper 1823). Walt Whitman, who in his poetry and prose exalted the spirituality of both cities and nature, wrote in his 1871 essay "From Democratic Vistas":

> . . . a new Literature, perhaps a new Metaphysics, certainly a new Poetry, are to be, in my opinion, the only sure and worthy supports and expressions of the American Democracy. Nature, true Nature, and the true idea of Nature, long absent, must, above all, become fully restored, enlarged and must furnish the pervading atmosphere to poems, and the test of all high literary and esthetic compositions. I do not mean the smooth walks, trimm'd hedges, poseys and nightinggales of the English poets, but the whole orb . . . (Foerster 1947:928).

The discovery of the natural environment as a cultural symbol of the "New Land" was the endeavor of a handful of individuals, albeit highly literate and scholarly men, who sensed the imminent destruction of the landscape by the rapid growth of the railroad and the development of cities following the 1850s, and they were primarily spokesmen for its preservation. By 1870 the population of Chicago was 300,000, where only 40 years before it had been counted as a mere 350; only ten years earlier, in 1860, railroads had clocked a mileage of 30,000, and the value of the country's manufacturers equaled that of its agricultural production (Foerster 1947:275).

Though the small group of literary and philosophic individuals were spokesmen for the preservation of the natural environment, in no sense were they a broad public movement, nor did one exist. Nevertheless, federal policy that led to the preservation and management of large tracts of land was drafted, first in 1849, with the establishment of the U.S. Department of the Interior, and then in 1872, of Yellowstone National Park.

No doubt the seminal work of George Perkins Marsh, Man and Nature (1864), which stressed the responsibility of human societies for the quality of their environment, had provided the ideology and philosophic rationale for land management decisions that followed; but the publication of Man and Nature was itself some four years prior to the organization of the Appalachian Mountain Club in 1876 and 20 years before the founding of the Sierra Club in 1892. These voluntary organizations embodied the ideology of preservationism and were, in fact, the inspiration of philosophic leaders such as John Muir, who founded the Sierra Club. The passage of land management legislation predated their organizational existence, however. In 1864, for example, Congress, in an unprecedented step, granted Yosemite Valley in California to the state to protect for public use.

The role of formal voluntary organizations as interest groups in the formation of public policy was just ahead in time. The Sierra Club, after all, registered a total of 182 charter members gathered from the ranks of professional and business people in the Greater San Francisco Bay Area and faculty members from the University of California when it was incorporated in 1892. Its purpose at that time was simply to visit the Sierra Nevadas and publish information about them.

The 50 years from midcentury to the turning point of the twentieth century was a developmental period for the establishment of two coexisting, and not mutually exclusive, movements: the establishment of voluntary organizations whose goals and ideologies were dedicated to the preservation of the wilderness, wildlife, natural resources, or a combination of these three; and the movement to enact federal or state policy toward the protection of large tracts of space.

The notion of preserving the wilderness could not be separated from the conflicting trend of industrial expansion. By 1900 the separate pathways of preservationism and industrial expansion were to meet and collide on national land use decisions. This was illustrated by the prolonged controversy over the flooding and damming of the Hetch Hetchy Valley in Yosemite National Park for the stated purpose of generating a water reservoir for the expanding city of San Francisco. When the decision to flood the valley was finally reached in 1913, against the active lobbying of preservationists such as Muir, the wilderness preservationists had splintered away from the resource conservationists over the question of multiple uses of land and water.

In summary, the earliest environmental movement in the United States developed from the ideologies and public policies of individuals and not organizations—individuals who served as the ideological leaders for the future. These leaders were responsible, philosophically, for the founding of voluntary organizations such as the National Audubon Society in 1905 and the Izaak Walton League in 1922 (some 50 years after the Appalachian Mountain Club). Their concern was the continuance of the natural environment, the preservation of the wilderness, though the focus may have varied from group to group as it did from one individual to the next. Their core of commonality was the concern for the impact of industrial expansion, not only on their land, but their status in society as well. The antiurban, antiindustrial growth stance was reflective of a social strata whose wealth predated the rise of modern industrialism. The discussion of the involvement of the "old urban wealth" in the formation of land use interest groups and policies that follows will address itself to the issue of class and social policy.

SOCIAL CLASS AND SOCIAL POLICY

The formation of social policy with respect to the environment reached a level of conflict and political engagement at the turn of the century and was the product of certain cross-currents. Old upper class wealth viewed the growth of industrialization, the bureaucratization of business and labor, and the concurrent decline of small-scale agriculture and agriculturally centered rural communities as a continuous change in the U.S. social structure. The organization of industry and of labor into unions brought new structures into the society that threatened the traditional concept of the independent, self-made man, and, more importantly, gave rise to competing power structures. Political decisions no longer came as a result of rational action by intelligent men but involved a crude power struggle dominated by privileged wealth and effective city machines (Hays 1972).

Preservation or conservation, then, was viewed as a means of limiting industrial growth and the social change this would generate. It placed emphasis upon nature and the countryside rather than the socially unstable cities. The new converts to conservation between 1908 and 1910 were middle and upper income urban dwellers. The financing and leadership came from urbanites active in other types of urban reform. Hays (1972) points out that prominent conservationists such as William Kent and Walter L. Fisher had played important roles in the campaign of the Chicago Municipal Voters League for reform in government in the city. Those interested in reform of big city machines were also endorsing conservationism. Moreover, the Daughters of the American Revolution (DAR) maintained a special committee on conservation.

It is important to note, however, that they were focusing on saving western lands, areas far removed from the focus of cities or urban settings. The issue of preserving open land within urban settings comes much later in time, with the Pine Barrens a current illustration.

By the end of the first decade of the twentieth century, upper income urban dwellers had mustered together reformists from the ranks of the socially conscious voluntary organizations, such as the DAR, to endorse the resource preservation policies of Teddy Roosevelt and Gifford Pinchot. (Pinchot's mother, in fact, had been chairman of a DAR conservation committee.)

PRESERVATIONISTS AND CONSERVATIONISTS

The earlier preservation movement headed by John Muir and his followers in the Sierra Club had as its base an ideology of antimaterialism as expressed in the philosophy of Thoreau. This was subsequently linked to the early American concept of rugged individualism, as personified by frontiersman Natty Bumppo. In effect, preservationists were attempting to preserve eighteenth-century American culture and values, whether real or fictional, and formulating twentieth-century public policy in order to do so.

Concurrently, federal policy had focused on the need for the conservation of natural resources in the framework of utilitarianism. Dissimilar motivations by Pinchot and Roosevelt, the visionaries of federal conservation policy, were to cultivate this sentiment to obtain the support of the urban old wealth now needed to enact their federal legislation.

Thus began the American merger of support for federal resource conservation policy by old, preindustrial upper class political support. It was a marriage of convenience, certainly for the voluntary groups, since to limit growth of one giant—big business (and a growing big labor)—would support the growth of an equally expanding giant—that of the federal administration. However, they had chosen their alignments on the basis of their ability to influence and contain fewer public agencies that could in turn be used to contain the private industrial sector. They were joined in their concerns, though not politically, by the small, rural com-

munities who received few benefits and some disadvantages from
the new industrial society.

AGRICULTURAL POPULISM AND THE RUGGED INDIVIDUALIST

While the upper classes were fostering the myth of the rugged
individual, the farmers persisted in attempting to apply its ideology.
The philosophic basis of agricultural idealism came from its chief
U.S. proponent, Thomas Jefferson. The idea of democracy that he
posed was based upon the independence of the individual, or the
smallest unit of society, the family. The agricultural ideal was
the family farm owned by the men who operated it; and farm operators who were self-reliant and had the autonomy to make their
own decisions. The focus on independent decision making by the
smallest possible unit of society was in vivid contrast to the centralizing and bureaucratizing tendencies of the industrial society.

The small, independent farmer was the hero of the American
populist movement, while the giants of industry and government
were defined as threats to the autonomy of the rural existence.
Both the small farmers and the urban upper classes were concerned
about the "bigness" of business. They could indeed be swallowed
up in the sweep of cities and factories, but the farmers were
equally concerned with the "bigness" of government, except later
when it represented their interests in price supports. Yet their
quiet rural existence was to be reshaped by the industrialization of
agriculture after more than 50 years of technological development.
Agricultural and political interests became more like those of big
business, which farming had become, though the ideology of populism, of the autonomous, rugged individual, lingered on.

GROWTH AND CONTAINMENT

The central theme of environmental conflicts throughout the
history of the movement has been the question of containment and
control of industrial growth. Even when this is not the manifest
goal of environmental groups, it is certainly the outcome of
preservation policies.

The environmental conflict that gathered new momentum in
the 1960s drew from two value systems set on a collision course
throughout the last 125 to 200 years. The first was an ever-expanding concept of economic growth boosted by the introduction
of automation and technology, and made possible structurally

through complex bureaucratic systems in the business and governmental sector; the second was a new middle class with the political and financial means to fight for their image of a proper social environment, which has begun to defy and to alter the process of planning and attempts to enter and control the planning process.

RELEVANT ASPECTS OF LAND USE THEORY

The theories of land use planning that are most applicable to the aims of this research are those that deal specifically with the planning and politics of urban open space. The urban setting within which the Pine Barrens is couched is a major factor in the evolvement of land use controversies at a given point in time. Suburban sprawl and the negative consequences of megalopolis became evident on the Northeastern seaboard as late as the 1960s. However, at the onset, this research rejects the assumption that urban sprawl is the inevitable consequence of economic development in the New York-New Jersey region. The recent regional planning efforts in the Hudson basin show that there remains the possibility of preserving thousands of relatively undeveloped agricultural and upland tracts on the region's periphery. The Regional Plan Association's Mid Hudson Plan (1974) and the Rockefeller Foundation Hudson Basin Project (1975) both emphasize the importance of land use planning in the less densely urbanized areas north of New York City and beyond the industrial cities of New Jersey.

The basic assumption of these regional research and planning efforts is that the natural areas outside cities should be preserved as a "green drop" in which the values of the natural environment are ascendant, and in which land use policies prevent the sale and subdivision of the land for more dense human settlement. Of course, this has been central in the work of most regional planners: those for whom the preservation of "greenbelts" was elevated to a first principle of planning; and to those like William H. Whyte for whom peripheral green areas are only one type of natural landscape worthy of preservation by a number of possible means. Thus, the most important issue that guides the present research is not why large tracts of land (and water) should be preserved, but how and for what present and future purposes.

The question of how natural lands outside the cities may be preserved is nevertheless difficult to separate from the question of what cultural definition we assign to urbanized land. As a report of the Council on Environmental Quality (CEQ) pointed out in 1971, it is only relatively recently that we have begun to assign multiple values to land and water:

Basically, we are drawing away from the 19th-century
idea that land's only function is to enable its owner to
make money. One example of this change in attitude
is that wetlands, which were once characterized as
"useless," are now thought of as having "value."
As we increasingly understand the science of ecology
and the web of connections between the use of any
particular piece of land and the impact on the environment as a whole we increasingly see the need
to protect wetlands and other areas that were formerly ignored. This concern over the interrelated-
ness of land uses has led to a recognition of the need
to deal with entire ecological systems rather than
small segments of them (Bosselman and Callies 1971:34).

Despite the recent trend toward federal and state land use legislation, the Coastal Zone Management Act was not passed until 1972. The conflict between the value of land as an immediately marketable commodity and land as the basic element of an enduring ecosystem continues and is generally found to remain quite central in planning issues. This is true even in cases where land has ostensibly been removed from the market. The conflicts have a significance that is more general than even the controversy over allocation of land uses, for as David Sills (1975:36) states:

This confrontation of ideologies and organizations
illustrates the point that in conflicts and debates over
what are the proper priorities, over what rights individuals, corporations, and minorities have to enjoy,
protect, utilize, or destroy the environment, the
quality of life in the society of the future may be
largely determined.

The removal of important tracts of land from the market generally requires some transfer of title to a public agency as well as some legislative determination of the future status of private in-holdings. For this reason the politics of use versus preservation are intimately linked to the public agencies that are brought into the controversy by the actions of various citizen interest groups (Klausner 1971:90). This observation establishes the dimensions of the historical study. It was important to analyze in some detail the history of public and government involvement in the issues.

Removal of land areas from the private sector is merely the beginning of planning for preservation and use. Except in the relatively unique case of wilderness designation—generally for tracts quite removed from major cities—land that is removed from the market must be designated for some other socially desirable use. In or near urban regions, woodland and abandoned farmland is viewed in the negative sense as "wasteland." Thus Whyte's (1968:181) criticism of urban greenbelts is relevant in this regard:

> There is, in short, too much vacuum. Where land has been purchased for public recreation there is little danger of encroachment. Where it has not been, which is to say in most of the green belts, the pressures for conversion to other uses are becoming increasingly difficult to stave off. The problem is not the easy one of commercial blight versus open space. Competition comes from other good uses, housing especially, and in the clash of causes the tangible has a strong edge over the intangible.

A number of important experimental land use planning policies, such as land banking and the leasing of agricultural lands to their original owners by states and countries, attempt to avoid the problem of nonuse without conversion to recreational uses. Unfortunately, these and similar experiments are outside the scope of this research, though planning systems for the preservation of the Pine Barrens are noted as they relate to the history and development of open-space policies. Recent legislation designed to deal with the complexity of Pine Barrens management systems is included as the structure from which interest groups and coalitions are formed. The Pine Barrens Coalition, for example, formed in 1977, cites as one of its goals the passage of HR6625, a bill introduced by Congressman James Florio. This legislation (which was followed by two remarkably similar proposals by other New Jersey legislators and a third attempt to legislate preservation through a bond issue) was drafted as a means of establishing a National Ecological Reserve through the concept of "green-line boundaries."

Although the coalition lists a membership of diverse conservation and environmental organizations already participating in the environmental decision-making process, conflict within this new coalition stems from varied interpretations of acceptable land management levels of control. While "old-line conservationists" support restricted federal intervention, "new-line environmentalists" emphasize greater federal management and restricted local control. This splintering of land management concepts serves to shape the legislation that is ultimately presented. Public hearings on proposed legislation and environmental regulations reflect the growing division within environmental groups, to say nothing of the opposing views among businessmen, farmers, local officials, and the legislators who represent them.

This "pluralism" among broadly defined environmental groups is discussed later in Chapters 3, 4, and 5 when the basis of interest-group information is explored.

In summary, then, as the states and federal government embark on the study of more than 20 proposed urban-area national parks, the relevance of empirical case studies is enhanced. The development of interest groups and their intervention in the drafting of management plans serve as significant data on the question of preserving open space in urban regions. In addition, even when there is a clear federal mandate for the preservation of a natural area outside an urban center, this does not end the controversy over planning.

Research conducted for the National Park Service by the author confirms the observation by Whyte and other planners that exemption of land from the market economy only marks the beginning of a new phase of conflict and accommodation (Goldstein 1975). Later phases of land use planning are always dependent on institutional arrangements made earlier, but the actual allocation of resources for public use raises new issues as to who shall be the beneficiaries of these policies and who shall change their traditional life style. It also raises new resource management issues. Included are those issues centering on carrying capacities and resource impact. This aspect of land use planning receives major attention in this Pine Barrens research.

BACKGROUND AND HYPOTHESIS

Settlement of any of the major issues that determine the fate of a natural area hinges on the processes of interest-group negotiation, political pressure, trade-offs, and emerging consensus. This study involves federal, state, and local agencies, as well as such an array of interest groups such as cranberry and blueberry farmers, local planning bodies, county freeholders, and varying kinds of conservation and environmental organizations. The range of negotiations and decision making in the planning process is thus highly complex. The type of emergent consensus or pressure group processes whereby conflict generates planning policies is the primary focus of this study. It must be emphasized, however, that this is a study in which the description of social processes is of primary interest. Consequently, the hypothesis guiding the collection of data is focused upon the social and political interaction generated by participation in interest groups.

A major hypothesis by the author guides the collection and analysis of data: As urbanized regions become the focus of environmental conflicts, a wider range of social class groups become involved.

Since the roots of the environmental movement in the United States are traced back to the conservation and preservation interest groups at the turn of the century (Nash 1973; Hays 1972; Marx 1964), and to the upper class old wealth (Hays 1972), the proponents of conservation and preservation have carried a tradition and image of elitism. Concern for the preservation of nature and the environment was considered a luxury of the established wealth. Further regions over which environmental conflicts ensued—Hetch Hetchy, for example—were wilderness areas remote from the sight or sound of less mobile citizens. In recent decades, however, particularly since the technological advance generated by the "machine" of World War II (Bensman and Vidich 1971), industrialization has forced changes upon the open landscape as well as upon urban neighborhoods. The more industrialization has changed the geography of urban regions, the greater has been the impact of planning decisions upon the life style of the communities within these regions. Interest-group participation in environmental conflicts has moved downward in social class since the turn of the century, adding some of the ranks of the middle classes to the growing membership in voluntary associations devoted to improvement or preservation of some aspect of the environment (Sills 1975; Morrison et al. 1972). This interest-group participation in urban regions now includes the involvement, at varying levels of activism, of relatively low income citizens responding to technological developments with social consequences in urban neighborhoods (Guseman and Hall 1977).

Although participation in interest groups has moved downward in social class since the turn of the century, leadership in interest groups continues to reflect the highest social class and educational background of those who participate. Participation and leadership may continue to reflect mutually exclusive social groupings. Guseman and Hall's (1977) study of a Houston black community's response to a proposed freeway extension sought to identify local leadership in terms of social class and education and concluded that leaders evidenced higher socioeconomic statuses.

While participation and pluralism reflect the kinds and numbers of interest groups centering on a particular issue, the enactment of environmental legislation in general has served to shift the planning and management power toward centralized public institutions, toward state and federal agencies, and away from local, private landholders and management, shifting its base from local government and the local elites that control government. The result is that land management and policy become a national issue as the attempt is made to preserve open spaces.

Moreover, while the centralization of all institutions, both public and private, by the 1970s placed land management disputes at the interface of big business and big government, it is smaller groups and individuals who act out the human drama. Recent Pine Barrens land ownership investigations, for example, revealed that several major banks were behind recent private land acquisitions and holdings. The irony of such an arrangement is best understood against the backdrop of rural populism that governs the ideology of local interest groups discussed in depth in Chapter 5. However, despite the issue of corporate control and conflict, land use planning is nevertheless forged by the social action and processes of interest groups and individuals. It is therefore necessary to study interest-group formation, leadership formation, and the political networks to and by which they interconnect.

FINDING AND ASSESSING INFORMATION

The methods used for the identification of interest groups and their networks of participation were primarily participant observation with the addition of historical research and the analysis of existing qualitative data. The focus of the research was twofold: to identify the role and participation of interest groups in forging public policy; and to place them within the larger historical, social, economic, and political context that serves to determine the fate of an immense tract of open land within a highly urbanized region.

Participant observation involved attendance at the seemingly endless public hearings conducted by the Department of Environmental Protection concerning the regulations for upgrading of water quality standards, many of which were conducted in local school gymnasiums in the Pine Barrens where between 50 and 100 persons testified at length over a five- or six-hour period. In later meetings, participation included the presentation of testimony before congressional subcommittees, both in the Pines and in Washington, D.C., on proposed legislation.

In addition, participant observation covered the range of informal gathering with individuals and groups representing various interest factions. Two Pine Barrens families (a cranberry grower and a local mayor) offered overnight hospitality, both of whom provided informal opportunities to observe life styles and values of long-time residents. Similarly, attendance at "Piney" folk music gatherings and picnics permitted observation of culture and life style of these unique Pine Barrens residents, while numerous interviews included taping of country music as well.

Interviews were conducted with relevant informants on the federal, state, and local government levels, including New Jersey Governor Brendan Byrne, Congressman James Florio, Congresswoman Millicent Fenwick, Congressman Frank Thompson Jr., Assemblyman Charles Yates, Mayor Floyd West. Although for health reasons, Congressman Edwin Forsythe was unable to fulfill an interview, his staff provided four hours of tapes from a Pine Barrens conference.

Further interviews included the commissioner of agriculture, deputy commissioners of environmental protection, former commissioners of transportation, labor, and industry, prosecutors in the attorney general's office, the director of the Bureau of Outdoor Recreation of the Department of the Interior, leaders and representatives of local planning bodies, including J. Garfield DeMarco, chairman of the Pinelands Environmental Council (PEC), and several conservationists who were members of the PEC.

The list of persons interviewed for this study is almost too long to itemize. It includes farmers who represent the New Jersey cranberry and blueberry industry, mayors of local townships, local county planners, representatives of various conservation and environmental organizations, the Pinelands Cultural Society, and local radio and newspaper journalists.

The purpose of these interviews and observations was to identify relevant interest groups and leaders, to determine the basis of their ideological differences, and to evaluate the overall impact of these components on planning goals, processes, and outcomes.

The historical analysis required a search of literature on the historical records and documents that cover the 300 years of history related in Chapter 1. Here analysis raised the question: How did a rural region retain its character in the midst of a rapidly industrializing era and region?

Interviews and content analysis of planning documents, master plans, and legislation provided data for Chapter 3 on the jetport controversy. The latter era, that of the 1970s, is ongoing and reached a political climax in 1980 as a key campaign issue of the New Jersey gubernatorial election. In this sense, the research was live in that it took place while the event was in progress. Moreover, in the second year of field work, the author entered into a participatory role with respect to planning and management organizations, serving as a member of the newly formed Pine Barrens Coalition. Later she was appointed by the governor to serve on the Pinelands Review Committee, and was requested by Congressman Florio to serve as expert witness before hearings of the House Interior Subcommittee and by Congressman Forsythe to serve in a similar capacity before the Fish and Wildlife Subcommittee.

The content of the study thus centers on a twofold focus as previously noted: to identify the role and participation of interest groups in forming environmental policy; and to place within an historical context the social, economic, and political institutions and trends that serve to determine the basis of interest-group formation. The second point in turn may serve as well to help us understand the fate of an immense tract of open land, a natural resource located within a highly urbanized region in the northeastern United States. To that research end the study is developed along the following chapter organization.

Chapter 1, "Early Settlements and Technological Change," examines the question of historical change. This chapter serves to explain not why the region has changed over the past 300 years, but the contrary: why it was not transformed into cities and factories as were most of the surrounding regions in New Jersey, Pennsylvania, and New York. Since the natural state of the Pine Barrens is a key factor in the conflict over land use and land use planning, the historical portrait of a rural setting provides the framework for social arrangements and networks that act upon modern disputes and interest group formations.

Chapter 2, "Human Settlements: People of the Pines," looks at three distinct groups of people who have settled in the region: the Pineys, the woods people; the farmers, including cranberry and blueberry growers, small businessmen, and townspeople; and the newcomers: the residents of leisure villages and new housing settlements. This chapter focuses on the question of social and political engagement in environmental decision making on the part of each of these groups and the history that has made them participants or nonparticipants in the struggle for land use control.

In Chapter 3, "The Pine Barrens in the 1960s: Conflicts between Conservation and Development Policies," post-World War II Pine Barrens is explored through the emergence of environmental conflicts. These conflicts coincide with a technological revolution spurred by the development of new technologies that began to transform isolated rural communities. Modern environmental conflicts begin with the 1960s, the proposed jetport and a New City planned for 200,000 people. This chapter examines the emergence of suburban interest groups and their impact upon political structures within state government. Chapter 4, "Water and Land: Cranberries and Housing," focuses upon the natural resources as motivation for conflict over control.

Chapter 5, "Cleavage and Organizational Strategy," centers on the transformation of interest groups into planning bodies and on the development of specific planning goals and ends. The second era of conflict brings together the divergent goals and plans of farmers, state and local officials, federal agencies, legislators, politicians, conservationists, and environmentalists into an ever-expanding pluralism. New interest groups are identified and political alignments sorted out and analyzed.

The question of social planning decisions in land use is posed against the ideology of the individual and of voluntary land management. In light of these considerations of land use systems, Chapter 6, "Emerging Institutional Arrangements for Land Use Policies," returns to the Pine Barrens and discusses land and water regulations and the growing drafts of legislation that attempt to forge and institute local, state, and federal land use policies. The emerging pattern of local (and therefore individual) control in rigorous conflict with larger-scale social planning by higher levels of government agencies is presented in the concluding chapter.

"The Land Ethic and Social Change," Chapter 7, examines those social and political formations that have helped to shape the land use conflicts and public policies of the Northeast, urbanized regions, and in particular the Pine Barrens. Beginning with the turn-of-the century formation of public policy on conservation and preservation issues, this chapter traces the emerging pluralism of interest groups and the downward shift in social class participation as industrialization and suburban growth overtakes older agricultural systems and affects rural, agricultural societies within the region.

PART I

POPULATION AND THE HUMAN ECOLOGY OF THE PINE BARRENS

INTRODUCTION TO PART I

Part I of this study presents the social and ecological setting of the evolvement of the Pine Barrens and the people of the Pines within a historical perspective. Its 300-year history, beginning with the rural isolation of the seventeenth century, entails the growth and subsequent decline of industrial development in the nineteenth century. Patterns of land use and life styles that emerged during this industrial decline set the stage for the 1960s, when a variety of interest groups began to organize in the Pine Barrens and to struggle over emerging issues of conservation and development. The isolation of the region was ultimately penetrated by commercial and industrial expansion and suburbanization within the Northeast region. The response to these changes is the formation of interest groups and activities that sought to limit or expand the commercial conversion of farmland and woodland.

1

EARLY SETTLEMENTS AND TECHNOLOGICAL CHANGE

> . . . [the land] is replenished with the goodliest
> woods of oaks and all timbers for ships and masts,
> mulberries, sweet cypresse, pines and firres. . . .
>
> Heston 1924

This description of the Province of New Albion, now known as South Jersey, was published in London in 1648, and with a few exceptions, the seventeenth-century observations continue to be reported of the Pine Barrens region today. The forests, the rich woods of oak, pine, and cypress, have been exalted in writing for at least 300 years. In 1680, for example, a Quaker named Mahlon Stacy wrote from Burlington (New Jersey) to his family in England:

> We have from the time called May to Michaelmas great
> store of very wild fruits, as strawberries, cranberries,
> and hortleberries, which are like our blueberries in
> England. . . . Indeed, the country take it as a wilderness is a brave country . . . and more wood than some
> would have upon their land (Heston 1924:11).

More than 200 years later, Gustave Kobbe (1889:85) described the same countryside as the wilderness Stacy detailed in his New Jersey correspondence with only the hint of human settlements:

> The Pines are the wildest portion of the State and except for the settlements along the railroad, the forest
> is broken only by a few lonely roads, almost abandoned
> old-time stage routes and lumber tracks; by narrow,
> swift, resinous-colored streams flowing silently through

> the colonnades of pines, or the gloomy labyrinths of
> cedar swamps toward the system of bays to the
> east. . . .

Finally, McPhee's (1967:1) opening passage in The Pine Barrens entitled "The Woods from Hog Wallow," describes a wilderness that is still omnipresent:

> . . . forest land reaches to the horizon. The trees are
> mainly oaks and pines, and the pines predominate.
> Occasionally, there are long, dark, serrated stands of
> Atlantic white cedars, so tall and so closely set that
> they seem to spread against the sky on the ridges of
> hills, when in fact they grow along streams that flow
> through the forest.

How a wilderness can be tucked within the southern corridor of the most industrialized state in the nation requires explanation that must be found in the 300 years of its recorded history.

Just how does a region, neatly set within the Northeast corridor between Boston and Washington, sustain a low population density (approximately two people per 100 acres) within a natural area of some 650,000 acres? By what plan or perhaps unintended consequences has the Pine Barrens region seemingly bypassed twentieth-century industrialization, the development of cities, and even of towns of 10,000 or more citizens, and remained a wilderness? The answers to these questions begin with the description of the geographic, social, and political boundaries of the Pine Barrens.

BOUNDARIES

The Piney region is an island of sand, swamp, and scrub timber isolated between the rich alluvial truck-farming district along the Delaware River and the bustling and prosperous seashore resorts (Halpert 1947:15). Its geographic boundaries cut across at least two southern New Jersey counties, Burlington and Ocean, and can be defined by the criteria of vegetation, the flow of rivers, or by roads and highways, depending upon the person employing the criteria. Some point out that isolation itself defines the parameters of the Pines. They suggest that "if there are no houses, you can yell and nobody hears you—that definition fits the Pine Barrens." Thus Assemblyman Doyle, who has spent some of his time exploring the Pine Barrens, raised this question:

> What is the Pines? No one agrees on a geographic
> definition. I've always defined it geographically—
> not according to flora. It's bounded by Route 206,
> 70, Black Horse Pike in the South, and the Garden
> State Parkway. I realize that's a little broad. On
> a road map it's the biggest white spot in the state.*

J. Garfield DeMarco, a major cranberry grower and chairman of the Pinelands Environmental Council, agrees that if flora were the criterion of boundaries, it would include all of South Jersey; but he chooses rivers and roads as parameters.

Sam Hunt, a Piney resident, described the Pine Barrens as emanating from its center, the Forked River Mountains: "Well, you're right in the middle of it. Whichever you goes. You goes to the south, you go to the West, you get to the Parkway, you'll go 20 miles West and you'll still be in the Pine Barrens."

Roughly speaking, the Pines covers one-third of the state and includes a narrow strip of land in Monmouth County just south of a rich farming belt, nearly all of Ocean County, and the eastern part of Burlington County, with portions of Camden, Salem, and Atlantic counties. The entire region continues south of the Mullica River, which in itself forms a boundary based upon soil composition and historic development.

According to land use potential for agriculture, the area north of the Mullica River watershed is considered distinct from the area to the south. North of the river the Lakewood Sand is the poorest, low in organic matter and mineral content, while in the area to the south Sassafras soils predominate. Moreover, transportation is more developed in the south along the route from Philadelphia to Atlantic City (Halpert 1947:16).

These two environmental distinctions, the potentiality of the soil to support agricultural development and the accessibility of transportation to centers of commerce and industry, have contributed to the stasis of the region over the period of its recorded history.

Heston (1924:201) comments on the timelessness of the geology and the traditions that comprise the environment:

---

*Quotations from people, identified as assemblyman or other such descriptions and not given a reference in the name-date style used throughout the book, come from personal interviews conducted by the author. They have not been given a reference to prevent repetitions.

> Here on the same rolling hills as elsewhere in South
> Jersey, with apparently the same soil, is a stunted
> growth of pine, laurel, vines and other scrubs such
> as might be found in Labrador or above the timber line
> on a mountain side. What causes it, no scientist has
> been able to tell. . . . The tradition is that the first
> white men found these Plains as they are today, and
> were told by the Indians that their traditions did not
> go beyond their presence.

For a working definition of the geographic limits of the Pine Barrens, we can select the official boundaries established by the legislation creating the Pinelands Environmental Council in January 1973. Labeled as "the Pinelands," the area designated is considerably smaller than had previously been defined and is limited to the lowest density, central part of Ocean County and a larger part of Burlington County. According to the Supplement to the PEC's Plan for the Pinelands (1975:63), the Pinelands region shall consist of the following:

> In Ocean County: All of Little Egg Harbor, Eagleswood, Stafford, Union, Ocean and Lacey Townships located westwardly of the Garden State Parkway, all of Manchester Township lying within the Lebanon State Forest, and all additional portions of Manchester Township lying southwardly of the line of right-of-way of the Toms River Branch of the Penn Central Railroad running westwardly from its junction with the Berkeley Township line to the Fort Dix Military Reservation boundary, and thence westwardly along the southern boundary of the military reservation to the Lebanon State Forest.
> In Burlington County: All of Washington and Bass River Townships, all of Medford, Shamong and Tabernacle Townships lying within the Wharton State Forest, and all of Pemberton Township lying within the Lebanon State Forest. Also included would be all of Woodland-Tabernacle township line and Burlington County Route 532 to the center of the Four Mile Circle.

What this amounts to is the most sparsely populated part of the Pine Barrens. Approximately 320,000 acres are included, about one-fourth of the state. Map 1 illustrates the portion of the Pinelands as the core of a much larger region if the region is defined by vegetation alone.

MAP 1

The Pine Barrens and the Northeast

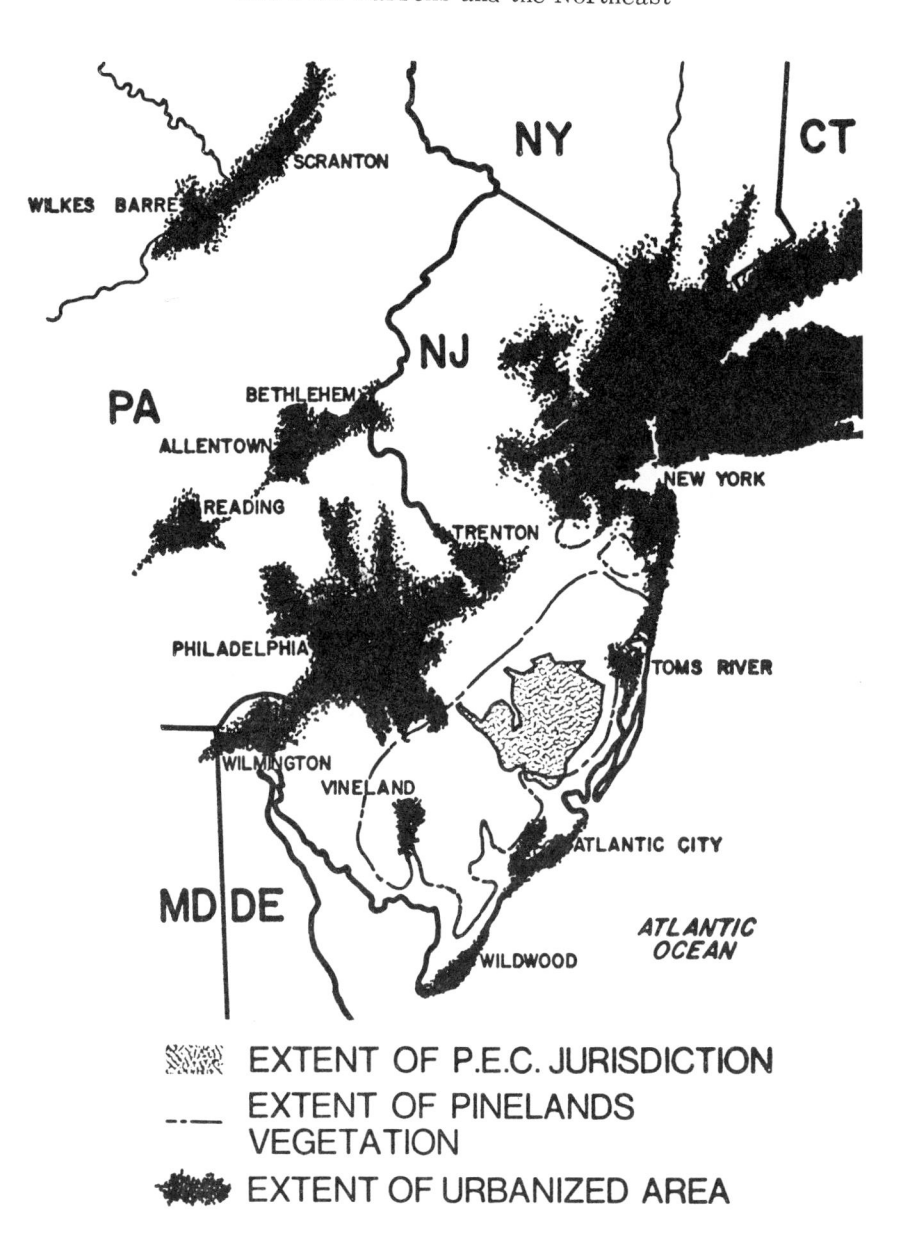

EXTENT OF P.E.C. JURISDICTION
--- EXTENT OF PINELANDS VEGETATION
EXTENT OF URBANIZED AREA

Source: Pinelands Environmental Council, Plan for the Pinelands (Philadelphia: Meridian Engineering, 1975).

The "official" boundary is also the most political, social, and economic boundary, based not on rivers or roads or on the low Forked River Mountain, but on ownership, power, and availability of open space for development.

Before we can understand the politics of these boundaries, the history of the region must serve to explain the unique condition of the Pine Barrens and its people.

EARLY HISTORY

Indians

Though the early presence of Indian settlements cannot be fixed in time, their absence from the landscape came soon after the first white settlers began to trade land rights for "worthless trinkets," not unlike the famous purchase of Manhattan. The white settlers of the Pine Barrens region who appear to have begun to settle on the fertile knolls along the bays and streams between the years 1665 and 1700 found evidence of previous inhabitants, but only small numbers of Indians. Their style of living with the land and the seasons by cultivating native corn (maize) and beans, fishing for clams and oysters, hunting deer, rabbits, partridge, quail, prairie chicken, and wild fowl was lost for the Indians when they exchanged land rights, giving way to a European cultural system of land ownership that restricted its use. Though they did not pursue a line of active resistance (or none that Quaker records describe) the Edge-Pillock tribe of the Delawares became part of the first Indian reservation in the country at Indian Mills in Burlington County, just across the Ocean County line. By 1802 the Delawares ceded their lands to the state of New Jersey and were removed to the Oneida Reservation in New York State (Heston 1924:204).

In many respects, throughout the seventeenth, eighteenth, nineteenth, and twentieth centuries, residents of the region, and particularly people who live in the woods, the Pineys, have retained the Indian life style of living with the land and the seasons; but only the names of some creeks and rivers serve as signposts of the early Indian existence: Manahawkin, Manasquan, and Westeconk (Heston 1924:204). Descendants of some Delaware Indians remained in the Pines, but their social organization and identity and their histories became virtually indistinguishable from other groups who came afterward.

Heston comments that there are still families among the old residents "in whose straight black hair, keen black eyes, swarthy skin and high cheekbones are evidence to back up the family tradition of Indian blood . . ." (Heston 1924:205).

Gladys Eayre, a current Piney resident, relates the following tale of her family history, which suggests that Indians were not so much eliminated as erased from white family histories.

> Family came in the late 1600s. I don't think they made the Mayflower, but my father's ancestors were sea captains originally and they came here from the whaling industry. They see a place so they stop. Some stayed on the shore and some went inland. The one that stayed on the shore, he went inland too—he married an Indian. And we can't find any record of him—he was blackballed—he came down here to live. There's all the other names but his. They just took his name right off the record.

Quakers

Early Quaker records noted births, marriages, and deaths within Quaker settlements and provide the most detailed history of Little Egg Harbor Township. The area itself was settled by Quakers (or Friends) who had bought the land from the Quaker proprietors. In other areas the early settlers were squatters in the sense that they occupied the land without title. The first residents were whalemen from Long Island, after "oyle and bone," who in turn had moved southward from Nantucket and Martha's Vineyard. They tended to settle along the coastal areas.

The Quaker settlers in the seventeenth century were English, largely from the east coast of Monmouthshire. Some traveled along the Delaware River and landed in Quaker colonies along the bay region. Water—the sea and the river—was the main form of transportation and later was to serve as the source of transportation for commerce. Land travel was restricted to Indian trails, and coach transportation was hindered by the soft sandy roads.

Isolated farmsteads became hamlets during the years 1700 to 1740 while milldams and gristmills were built. Commerce centered on water transportation. Settlers could trade by boat with New York, shipping lumber, furs, salt fish, rye, Indian corn, oysters, and clams.

Though shipbuilding became an important industry in Little Egg Harbor, communities nevertheless remained small, isolated, and without the institutional development of churches and schools. Commenting on this frontier life style in 1745, the Reverend Thomas Thompson, who was sent to America as a missionary by the Society for the Propagation of the Gospel in Foreign Parts, wrote in his journal:

> From Manasquan, for twenty miles further on in the
> country, is all one pine forest. . . . The inhabitants
> are thinly scattered in regions of solid wood. Some
> are decent people who have lived in better places,
> but those who were born and bred here have neither
> religion nor manners, and do not know so much as a
> letter in a book. As Quakerism is the name under
> which all those in America shade themselves that
> have brought up to none, but would be thought to be
> of some religion so these poor people call themselves
> Quakers . . . (Heston 1924:310).

Low density of population, tiny hamlets, and poor roads kept the inland settlements from developing into towns. By the beginning of the American Revolution, what is now Ocean County consisted of a few hundred families, scattered along the bay, each with its own farm, now and then a blacksmith, tavern keep, shipbuilder, or merchant, but certainly not a church or pastor. The water network, by contrast, is an interweaving of rivers and bays. Part of the waters of Ocean County drain into the Atlantic Ocean via Barnegat Bay; part flow east to the Delaware, and some go west then south and join the Mullica River.

During the American Revolution, privateering involved preying on British ships, and Jersey boats were able to escape into the Mullica River and transport their goods to Philadelphia. Privateering was one more act of extraordinarily independent people who were themselves dissenters, rebellious against established religion in England or New England with its Puritan code, French Huguenots, or Baptist and Presbyterian dissenters (Heston 1924:217).

The American Revolution engaged the Quakers in the war and many turned away from their religion. Moreover, while the Church of England and the Presbyterian Church were the first to send missionaries into the Pines in Colonial days, neither church could gain a foothold to establish a building or a society.

The Presbyterian Church gained a toehold in 1841, but it was not until after the Civil War that the Episcopal Church established itself, and not until a decade later that the Catholic Church moved into the county. Methodist circuit riders traveled through the Pines and competed with the Mormon Church, which, in the first half of the nineteenth century, began meetings in a schoolhouse at New Egypt.

Isolation did not lend itself to the building of churches or schools, social institutions that grow with communities and provide social centers. Though commerce along waterways was central to the development of cities in Medieval Europe, neither towns nor cities were to develop in the Pines region because industry itself centered on inland rural activities such as fisheries, farming, trapping, and lumbering. These activities require small clusters of people, a family unit, carried out in or near the woods rather than in a town. Transportation and sale of these products would require an occasional trek through the woods, but the main day-to-day activities were in the forests and bays. The most permanent structures at this point were inns or hotels set along the old stage roads.

Taverns played a significantly different role in the eighteenth and nineteenth centuries, serving as the social center for town meetings, military training and recruiting, voting and polling headquarters, and finally as a dispensary of spirits (Fowler and Herbert 1976:5). While these inn-based centers of social and commercial life remained along the rivers and forests, separate towns were simply unnecessary to provide the setting for these functions of social interaction.

THE IRON FORGE INDUSTRY

The iron industry created forge settlements that provided iron ore for cannons during the American Revolution. Ships and schooners were needed to carry the pig iron to New York, and shipbuilding expanded as an industry.

The iron business resulted in the depletion of pinewood, the carving of some roads through the pines, and introduced the first forested industrialists to the region. Martha's Furnace was built in 1793 by Isaac Potts and was apparently named after his wife. It was located on the East Branch of the Wading River.

The entire Pine Barrens region on the Wading River and Mullica River watersheds, and around the headwaters of the Rancocas, was filled with prosperous furnace towns, but everything depended on the iron industry. Iron remained king until anthracite was discovered in Pennsylvania, and valuable deposits of iron ore proved better than the Jersey bog ores.

Methods of reducing this ore with anthracite-fired furnaces were perfected in about 1840. An iron industry started up immediately in Pennsylvania with which the bog ore industry could not compete. In ten years the South Jersey furnaces went out of blast for all times. As the land in the Pine Barrens was unable to support the population, the towns were deserted, schooner traffic fell, and the whole area reverted to a primitive state. All vestiges of towns have long since disappeared, though the paper and glass industries that grew up with the iron business hung on for a while longer.

In this sense, low density, stable populations and self-limiting industry have served to maintain low levels of development and a continuity over time that has been relatively undisturbed until the last decade. Industries, which might have germinated towns or cities, did not last. New immigrants were not attracted to the area; and resources were inevitably exhausted or overextended and market demands were met in other regions.

For example, shipbuilding receded when more trees were cut down than could be replaced in sufficient time to meet the demand, and the entire operation moved on to the forests of Maine. The iron industry reached its peak in the years immediately following the War of 1812 and then declined with the introduction of the railroad, which allowed for transportation of iron from the seemingly limitless supplies in Pennsylvania.

Once they had moved in a downward swing, the industries died, leaving behind the bare structures of ghost settlements throughout the Pines, and nothing replaced them. Martha's Furnace is now little more than a plot of ground. A mine and a half north is the Wading River ghost town, the paper mill town of Harrisville.

In summary, forge and furnace communities grew in Ocean and Burlington counties between 1791 and 1815, a period of 24 years, but by 1840 a better grade of iron ore was found in Pennsylvania that was free from sulfur and near large deposits of coal and limestone. In addition, improved methods of smelting were being utilized and, from 1864 to 1854, the conditions grew so critical that the industry disappeared. Charcoal burning, which had served as fuel for the iron industry, continued to serve energy needs of big cities between 1830 and 1840. New York City was asking for charcoal by the boatload during the peak of that operation. Once again, however, Pennsylvania absorbed the industry by producing coal in sufficient quantities to shift the energy use from charcoal to coal, and a second industry disappeared from the Pines. Glass manufacturing had an equally brief life. A plant known as the Atlantic Glass Works was erected and operated between 1851 and 1866.

Then came the railroad. The Raritan and Delaware Bay Railroad had been laid to Manchester. Wealthy sea captains of Toms River, Forked River, Waretown, and Barnegat started the Ocean County National Bank. A land boom rose at the conclusion of the Civil War and was snuffed out five or six years later in the panic of the 1870s.

Real estate speculators from Jersey City bought a tract of land at Toms River village and during 1869-71 sold off lots and built a large summer hotel on the river bank. This was the beginning of the tourist industry for Ocean County, while Burlington County was developing its cranberry industry.

Cranberries had been growing wild in the bogs since the time of the Indians, but it was not until after the Civil War and the demise of the forge and furnace industries that the culture of cranberries began in seriousness and a land boom began. Swampland was selling for $100 per acre until the panic of 1873, when the bottom dropped out of the boom.

For all practical purposes, the Pine Barrens had had its industrial revolution in the eighteenth century and was on a descendent path industrially as early as the mid-nineteenth century when other regions, particularly in Pennsylvania, were ascending. This was the result of several factors. Technological change continually moved beyond the resources of those who cultivated the region. Communities such as Harrisville were early company towns based on a single product that, when no longer viable, ended the economic and social basis of the town. Even in their prime, those forge furnace, paper, and glass towns were never self-sufficient. No secondary industries were developed. Significantly, the acid composition of the soil persistently defied agricultural development. In that sense, they were comparable to cities in their dependence upon an extended agricultural belt for their food; but unlike the large cities, these towns did not have a variety of products and industries to fall back on as technology shifted and their economy became obsolete. The small Pennsylvania mining towns, once rural and wooded like the Pine Barrens, became coal towns and later steel towns and moved in an industrial succession from which the Pine Barrens receded. In terms of time, the descendent economic path occurred within a 40-year span. Table 1 illustrates the rise and fall of the iron forge communities and the brief time span involved.

IMPACT OF INDUSTRIAL DECLINE

Population

The descendants of the glassworkers and the furnace workers had moved from these once-active settlements to live in small houses scattered through the Pines, in or near towns such as Brown's Mills or Chatsworth. Still others traveled farther to small towns in the farm belt just outside the district, to Buddtown, Magnolia, Cookstown, and New Egypt; or toward the shore in Ocean County to Tom's River, Waretown, and Tuckerton.

The census of 1905 compared with five years earlier shows a consistent decline in population in all townships and boroughs located within the current Pinelands boundary (State of New Jersey 1906). The numbers were small to begin with. Little Egg Harbor

TABLE 1

Iron Forge Communities in the New Jersey Pine Barrens

Community	Location	Inception	Decline
Burlington County			
Martha's Furnace	Wading River, 2 miles above Harrisville	1793	1847 to 1853
Hanover Furnace	Pemberton Township	1791	1847 to 1853
Speedwell	4 miles south of Chatsworth	1793	1847 to 1853
Wading River Forge and Slitting Mill	Harrisville	1793	1847 to 1853
Stafford Forge	New Mills, Pemberton	1800	1847 to 1853
Ocean County			
Federal Furnace	Lakehurst	1789	1847 to 1853
Ferrage (Bamber)	Bamber	1809	1847 to 1853
Dover Forge	4 miles from Ferrago	1809	1847 to 1853
Phoenix Forge	New Mills	1815	1847 to 1853

Source: Compiled by the author.

Township went down from 1,865 to 517 in that five-year period. Ten of the 14 townships show a population decline between 1875 and 1895, and, over a 50-year period, from 1855 to 1905, in each township where figures exist, the population was greater in 1855 than it was in 1905. Tables 2 and 3 present these data.

Those who had moved further into the woods were no doubt undercounted, and it is difficult to estimate the number of people who were or became "Pineys," those for whom a life style evolved in which a cycle of hunting and gathering ensued in the Pines. They hunted deer in the winter and gathered cranberries and blueberries and sold hay during other times of the year. They traded some of the fruits of their hunting and gathering but primarily lived in a subsistence economy. Their life style reflected that of the seventeenth century and the early Indians before the rise and fall of industries in the area.

It is at this point, at the decline of the industrial activity in the Pinelands region, that schemes to exploit the land and water begin to take root. In 1876 Joseph Wharton, a Philadelphia industrialist, purchased the Batsto Estate. After he gathered parcels of land until more than 96,000 acres had been accumulated, he proposed to pipe its voluminous ground water supply, the aquifer, to Philadelphia as a new source of water for that city, but the New Jersey legislature intervened and the project was shelved.

The state began acquiring lands in the Pine Barrens and creating public recreational areas. Lebanon State Forest was established in 1908 and covered 22,185 acres of forest land in Burlington and Ocean counties; then Bass River, 9,270 acres, was established in 1905 and Penn State, 2,958 acres, in 1910.

World War I brought an unexpected and abrupt change for the region and its people: Fort Dix was built in 1917. The building of this major military base (currently about 55 square miles) resulted in the dislocation of some of the people of the region. The fort also became a source of jobs for Pineys and Bayshackers (those who lived in the villages closer to the bay). "Uncle" Bill Britten was a carpenter for the military base; Gladys Eayre told of driving trucks for the army at the fort; and Sam Hunt worked for the state (actually the county) repairing roads. The introduction of the outside world through the presence of two military camps (the Lakehurst Naval Air Station was commissioned in 1921) brought down the seal of isolation for the region.

The use of the automobile brought a change in the system of transportation. Ocean County was no longer a seafaring community but a resort area. In the decade of 1910 to 1920, the neighborhood around Toms River grew rapidly; Ocean Gate, Pine Beach and Beachwood, Seaside Heights, Bay Head, and Mantaloking emerged

TABLE 2

Change in Pine Barrens Population, 1900-05

Township	1900	Percent	1905	Percent	Percent Difference
Burlington County					
Bass River	800	1.4	728	1.1	0.3
Medford	1,969	2.6	2,030	2.7	+0.1
Pemberton	1,493	2.5	1,706	2.7	+0.2
Shamong	910	1.6	508	0.8	0.8
Tabernacle*	—		462		
Washington	617	1.0	678	0.9	-0.1
Woodland	398	0.7	413	0.6	-0.1
County N =	58,211		62,042		
Ocean County					
Eagleswood	563	2.8	534	2.5	-0.3
Manchester	718	3.6	653	3.1	-0.5
Ocean	436	3.3	509	2.0	-0.2
Stafford	1,009	5.1	994	4.8	-0.3
Union	955	4.8	913	4.4	-0.4
Little Egg Harbor	1,856	9.4	517	3.6	-6.9
County N =	19,747		20,880		

*Incorporated in 1901.
Source: State of New Jersey, Department of State, Census Bureau, Compendium of Census 1726-1905 (New York: John L. Murphy Publishing Company, 1906).

TABLE 3

Change in Pine Barrens Population from Civil War to Turn of Century

Township	1860	1870	1880	1890	1900	Percent Difference
Burlington County						
Bass River	—	807	1,001	853	800	
Medford	2,136	2,189	1,980	1,864	1,969	-0.6
Pemberton	2,672	1,946	2,086	1,805	1,493	-2.5
Shamong	1,008	1,149	1,097	958	910	-0.3
Tabernacle	—	—	—	—	—	
Washington	1,728	609	889	310	617	
Woodland	—	389	325	327	398	-2.3
County N =	49,730	53,639	55,402	58,528	52,841	
Ocean County						
Eagleswood	—	—	592	791	563	
Lacy	—	—	814	711	718	
Manchester	—	1,102	1,057	1,057	1,033	
Ocean	—	—	—	—	—	
Stafford	—	—	484	482	436	
Union	1,918	1,923	1,024	1,063	955	-12.3
Little Egg Harbor	—	—	—	—	1,856	
County N =	11,176	13,628	14,455	15,974	19,747	

Source: State of New Jersey, Department of State, Census Bureau, Compendium of Census 1726-1905, together with Tabulated Returns of 1905 (New York: John L. Murphy Publishing Company, 1906).

35

as beach resort towns, though portions of these areas are not now considered part of the Pine Barrens. The census in Ocean County indicated a doubling of the population from 1850 to 1920, from 10,043 to 22,155.

One resident recalls the change: "At one time you could drive all the way from the Mullica River to Tom's River and never see a house."

The Pennsylvania Railroad extended its line from Whitings to Toms River and steamboats were put on Toms River to connect with Island Heights and Seaside Park.

Inland, however, the chief economic activity was agriculture, and agriculture was declining. The 1923 Soil Survey of the Chatsworth area reported a decreasing number of farms as farmers recognized that the land could support primarily cranberry and blueberry crops (Pinelands Environmental Council 1975:54). The question remained: How to make the land pay off financially? Lots were subdivided and sold to immigrants in cities during the 1920s to induce them to own "their piece of the country." During the 1930s much of the Pine Barrens was taken off the tax rolls—if it had ever been on. The state held certificates of tax liens. The so-called immigrant-owned land was understandably ignored, during the Depression, but as original owners began to die, their survivors were unaware of the earlier transactions. The result was spurious ownership, both by the state and private citizens. This led to schemes of land fraud that resulted in legal investigation in the 1970s when land once again held promise of yielding economic reward.

Summary

The fact that the Pine Barrens retains the characteristics of a wilderness is more the product of geographic and geologic factors that limited the subsequent social organization. Its social character is an unintended consequence of these delimitations.

Despite a 300-year history, neither cities, substantial towns, heavy industry, service industries, nor mixed agriculture are in evidence; but this result is not the product of rational planning and the policies of conservationists. It is much more the end result of trial and error and short-term planning on the part of businessmen, land speculators, and capitalists who did not have to oppose a conservation or ecology movement in order to overextend the resources. It was only in the 1960s and 1970s that social conflict and the politics of land use emerged to determine the ultimate fate of the Pine Barrens. Up until this point, the land itself has controlled the amount and direction of growth—or nongrowth—and, to that extent, the nature of the social organization of those who have lived within the Pinelands.

2

HUMAN SETTLEMENTS: PEOPLE OF THE PINES

In the West, you could always move on—if you didn't like your neighbors, you could always push on—push on. But here, there's no where else to go. I guess you could shut out the outside world cause you really can't see very far in the Pines. . . .

Within the structure of human settlements in the Pine Barrens region, there are at least three distinct groups of people. First are the Pineys, the woodspeople whose existence has been marked by a system of hunting and gathering and small-scale subsistence farming. The Pineys are part of the rural, Appalachian mountain pre-industrial society whose weathered and unpainted wooden houses sit far back into the woods. From the turn of the century onward, those few writers who had discovered the Pineys depicted them either in the nostalgia of the American Romantic movement (McPhee 1967; Halpert 1947) or in the brutally denigrating portrait of a rural "backward" people (Goddard 1913), a portrait whose social and political ramifications will be discussed later in this chapter.

The second distinct grouping consists of farmers, blueberry and cranberry growers (primarily), and small-scale businessmen whose family histories may date back to the early Quaker records of the seventeenth century or to the turn-of-the-century immigrants, the descendents of Italian migrant fruitpickers, many of whom live within or near the small villages. Finally, there are the newcomers, the suburbanites who have been flocking to the growing number of leisure village senior housing and cluster developments. They can be described as exurbanites or, more recently, exsuburbanites once again on the move.

The purpose of this chapter is to understand the composition of the human settlements as various groups interact more or less in the social and political arena of environmental decision making. It is not an attempt to portray in an anthropological sense the microsociety of the Pine Barrens. This indeed is the basis of another study at some given point in time. This chapter, however, places the human settlements in a social, historical, and political context that offers insights and understandings on the degree and kind of participation in environmental decision making that various Pine Barrens groups have generated toward the formation of land use planning. Therefore, these groups are distinguished from each other less by their national and historical roots and more by their life style and access, greater or lesser, to the benefits and power within the larger social system.

For example, in terms of political participation in policy formation, the farmers and small businessmen maintain the powerful decision-making roles, while the Pineys, already removed from the machinations of mass society for reasons explored in depth in the following pages, are themselves virtual nonparticipants.

The third group, the newcomers here referred to as suburbanites, form a political constituency for the local, existing power structure. Provided the newcomers' interests in low taxes are served, and also provided that significant services, such as health care, are considered in the planning process, this last group may continue to support the local factions in the election of officials and in the passage of bond issues. However, their numbers are large and a shift in local politics could conceivably activate in the opposite direction. For example, Ocean County now lists 26 retirement communities with an estimated population of 35,100. Burlington County, on the other hand, is less well developed, more geographically removed from the shore. Nevertheless, newcomers to the Burlington County Pine Barrens area (those who are not leisure village residents) have already participated in political fights for school board representation, and some have joined the recently formed southern chapter of the Sierra Club. This latter group, the West Jersey Sierra Club, has been moving in a collision course with local business-farmer interests on the question of growth and development of the region.

The following three sections of this chapter deal with the three distinct groupings of people in the Pines. As noted earlier in this chapter, the exploration of human settlements in the Pine Barrens is a study of the participants and nonparticipants as well as the marginal participants in the environmental decision-making process, which is, after all, the focus of this book. Moreover, while the role of active participants in Pine Barrens land use disputes has been described throughout this book, the social history behind the nonparticipation of the Piney is reflected upon primarily within this section alone. This group's alienation from the mass society at an earlier point in history sets the stage for their current nonparticipation and low representation in planning groups who speak in the name of the Pine Barrens. Piney nonparticipation, in turn, enhances the political hegemony of the active participants, the farmers and small businessmen, who comprise the socially and politically dominant force within the Pine Barrens.

THE PINEYS: ISOLATION AND POVERTY

Early in the twentieth century, the remote Pineys—who were reported to have been descended from runaway Hessian soldiers during the American Revolution; or runaway slaves from the South who, finding the forests of New Jersey, believed they had reached free Canada; or independent frontiersmen, privateers, and Indians—were themselves suddenly swept from their private world to the scrutinizing attention of eugenicists and public officials.

This attention was generated by the work of a psychologist and researcher, Henry Herbert Goddard. His post at the Vineland Training School for retarded children led to the search for "scientific" benchmarks of mental retardation and "feeblemindedness," as it was called, in Piney families, a work that culminated in the publication of The Kallikak Family (Goddard 1913).

In 1908, a sojourn to Europe led Goddard to the work of Alfred Binet and Henry Simon in Paris, and to the recently devised intelligence test. Armed with his newly acquired tool of intelligence measurement and a plethora of family history charts, similar in character to those devised by Mendel for his study of heredity in peas, Goddard sought to link heredity and feeblemindedness in this spurious case study of a Pine Barrens family. The Kallikak Family evolved from Goddard's study of the pseudonamed Deborah Kallikak, a child born in an almshouse and placed in the Vineland Training School for Feebleminded Boys and Girls.

The psychologist discovered that one branch of this family was (probably) illegitimately sired with a Piney tavern maid and produced scores of "feebleminded" and "sexually loose" descendents, while a second marriage to a woman of good upstanding citizenry, a North Jersey upper income family, produced judges and senators. From this analysis, Goddard was to conclude that Piney intelligence was rooted in their genes, and that those genes were apparently inferior.

This study, highly questionable in its scientific method and conclusions, was to bring stigma to the word and person of the Piney and create suspicion and remoteness toward the world outside the Pines. Not content to stigmatize the very real poverty of the Piney in the name of science, Goddard was to foster the idea of a "final solution" based on sterilization of the group. Thus, poverty was a sin for which society need accept no responsibility other than to eliminate the poor, rather than the source of poverty.

A disciple of Goddard's (Crissey 1977) comments with pride that group intelligence testing, such as the Binet test used by Goddard and the Army Alpha, were used for "delinquents, criminals, immigrants and school children." Of that diverse grouping, the psychologist Goddard (1913:71) theorized that it was "mentally defective people" who lived in and created slums:

> If all of the slum districts of our cities were removed tomorrow and model tenements built in their places, we would still have slums in a week's time, because we have these mentally defective people who can never be taught to live otherwise. . . . Not until we take care of this class and see to it that their lives are guided by intelligent people, shall we remove these sores from our social life.

The social Darwinist placed the cause of social ills generated by the emerging new industrial society upon the people most disadvantaged by these social changes. Thus Goddard (p. 71) concluded that population control of Pineys was an important innovation to social policy, no matter how that would be accomplished: "There are Kallikak families all about us. They are multiplying at twice the rate of the general population, and not until we recognize this fact, and work on this basis, will we begin to solve these social problems. . . ." What was it that Goddard had found in his study of the Kallikaks that led to this extreme position with respect to the isolated Pineys?

Fielding for Cultural Bias

Elizabeth Kite was the field worker for Goddard, and it was she who persistently tracked down the living members of Deborah Kallikak's family, then made a rapid, on-the-spot diagnosis of "feeblemindedness," and finally collected "hearsay" data about other living and dead relatives to form this composite portrait of a "degenerate family." It was these data that served as Goddard's scientific basis for the aforementioned conclusions. However, it was from the field observations of Elizabeth Kite, an upper class young woman who had spent a year in Paris at the Sorbonne and a year in London studying in the area of historical research and who had "infinite patience with the poor, . . ." that we are able to catch a glimpse of the poverty of the cabin people, though it is unlikely that Kite, with her privileged background, could recognize the manifestations of rural poverty. It is from Kite's labeling of rural poverty as "degenerate" and "feebleminded" that we come to understand the distrust and anger the Pineys felt toward the "helping" institutions of the larger society. For example, in the following passage (Goddard 1913:78), Kite depicts poverty but concludes feeblemindedness, as she describes the experience of a distressed Piney family:

> It was a bitter, cold day in February and about eleven in the morning when the field worker knocked at the door. Used as she was to sights of misery and degradation, she was hardly prepared for the spectacle within.
> The father, a strong, healthy, broad-shouldered man, was sitting helplessly in a corner. The mother, a pretty woman still, with remnants of ragged garments drawn about her, sat in a chair, the picture of despondency. Three children, scantily clad and with shoes that would barely hold together, stood about with drooping jaws and the unmistakable look of the feebleminded. . . . The boy with her wore an old suit that was evidently made to do service by night as well as by day. A glance sufficed to establish his mentality, which was low.

It is with glances and assumptions that Kite comes to the conclusion that the family is genetically feebleminded. She does not ask herself or the family she is assessing what relationship may exist between the socioeconomic condition and the abject poverty she has left in her record. Therefore, she presents data that vigorously support Goddard's notion of social Darwinism:

> The whole family was a living demonstration of the futility of trying to make desirable citizens from defective stock through making and enforcing compulsory education laws. Here were children who seldom went to school because they seldom had shoes. . . .
> The mother in her filth and rags was also a child. In this house of abject poverty, only one sure prospect was ahead, that it would produce more feeble-minded children with which to clog the wheels of human progress. . . . These and similar questions kept ringing through the field worker's mind as she made her way laboriously over the frozen road to the station. . .
> [p. 78].

42 / ENVIRONMENTAL DECISION MAKING

In another observation and field visit, we note the experience of a distressed Piney family with respect to health care and educational institutions in the society of early twentieth-century United States:

> Arrived at the farm, the question of the mentality of this family was quickly answered. Desolation and ruin became more apparent at every step. . . . She [the field worker] gazed aghast at what appeared to be a procession of imbeciles. The tall, emaciated, staggering man at the head braced himself against a tree, while the rest stopped and stood with a fixed, stupid stare. Quickly regaining control, the field worker said pleasantly, "Good morning, Mr. Saunders. I hope you don't mind my intruding on you this way, but you see I am looking up the children of the neighborhood, and I was sorry not to find any of yours in the Cedarhill school to-day."
>
> He at once thought he had to do with a school inspector, and his answer bears no setting forth in print. It was an incoherent, disjointed, explosive protest against school laws in general and fate in particular . . . [pp. 90-91].

When Kite acknowledges that fate had brought the death of the wife, she bears little understanding toward the desolation of the man or his sense of powerlessness in the face of impersonal institutions:

> The field worker began to feel sympathy for the man, although she knew that he was drunk and that drunkards are moved easily to tears. . . .
>
> "Yes she's dead!" he answered with a wild gesture, "they took her right out of that room—they said they'd cure her, if I'd let her go . . . they took her away and she never came back. Oh!" Stifling his sobs, he went on, "And now they say I am to send my children to school—and what can I do?" [p. 90].

The solution that Kite, representing the institutions of the larger society, offered the man was the option to remove his child to an institution, Goddard's institution, no doubt. In the following passage, we note the subjective bias Kite held toward the rural Pineys when she describes the young girl in the family: "A lump of humanity, a girl who, at first glance, had thrown her imbecile shadow over the whole group, making them all look imbecile. . . ." When the father describes the girl as a possible epileptic, "she's always falling into fits," we wonder why Kite did not probe the use and meaning of the word "fits" to determine what this might have been a description for; but for the field worker, this becomes an excellent opportunity to recruit the girl for the Vineland Training School: "Breaking in here, the field worker said, 'But Mr. Saunders, you ought not to have the burden and the care of that girl; she could be so happy and comfortable in a place where they understand such cases. You ought . . .'" [p. 90]. Before the field worker can continue with her pitch for institutionalization, the Piney defends his concern for keeping the family together. This concern is translated by Kite as "wild" and "desperate" behavior:

> The field worker could get no farther. His eyes suddenly assumed a wild, desperate look and he burst out, "No, no! They took my wife away and she never came back . . . they'll never get her . . ." and the field worker drove away, pondering deeply the meaning of what had been seen and heard [pp. 90-91].

The outcome of these ponderings for Kite and her mentor, Goddard, was a fairly popular theory of social Darwinism they referred to as the "Mendelian Law." Using Mendel's system for tracing the genetic distribution in peas from one generation to another, the psychologist Goddard charted Kallikak family trees based on hearsay, assumptions, and a good measure of social class discrimination. These data then laid the foundation for the proposed practice of genetically selective sterilization, as well as segregation of Piney families from the rest of society.

Both Goddard and Kite use the exact phrase "final solution" when they caution that, at best, "sterilization is not likely to be a final solution . . . until we can get segregation thoroughly established." That these theories seem to parallel concepts and language for racial targeting within Germany in the 1920s and 1930s is more than coincidental.

The Social Significance of Social Darwinism

In his study of the science and politics of I.Q. testing, Kamin (1974) makes the point that the establishment of the first usable test of general intelligence, published by Binet in 1905, attracted the interest of men with sociopolitical views, among them Goddard in New Jersey, Lewis Terman at Stanford, and Robert Yerkes at Harvard. To foster these views the eugenics movement at the turn of the century gained scientific legitimacy through the mental testing movement.

Hence, various minority groups were to be subjected to culture-laden intelligence testing and subsequently labeled "dull," or the more insidious term, "feebleminded."

While Terman singled out the Indian and Mexican children, and later blacks, Goddard focused on East European immigrants and the poor of southern New Jersey, people who for the most part were identified as Pineys.

To be diagnosed as "feebleminded" had significant social consequences in the early twentieth century, since distinctions between the criminal, the poor, the insane, and the "dull" were not clearly drawn (Kamin 1974). Not only could persons so labeled become institutionalized, they were subject to legalized sterilization in states where such laws were passed under the belief that heredity played a primary role in the transmission of crime, idiocy, and imbecility (Kamin, 1974:3).

The Social Consequences for Pineys

In 1913 the governor of New Jersey, James F. Fiedler, cited the report of Elizabeth Kite on the Piney family and subsequently proposed to "segregate New Jersey's Pineys."

The headline in the June 29, 1913, edition of the New York Sun noted that the governor found the Pineys a menace to the state. The subheadline continued in the best of yellow journalism: "Shocked at Conditions He Found in Race of Imbeciles, Criminals, Defectives in the Pine Belt of Burlington County." The news story covers the governor's journey through the Pine Belt, ending as his journey concludes at Brown's Mills Junction, a railroad stop in the midst of the Pinelands. The trek ends with the following summation of the "final solution" for Pineys. The governor states:

> . . . I have been shocked at the conditions I found. Evidently these people are a serious menace to the state of New Jersey. . . . They are inbred and lawless and lead scandalous lives till they have become a race of imbeciles, criminals and defectives. . . . The state must segregate them, that is certain. I think it may be necessary to sterilize some of them (New York Sun, June 29, 1913).

Not only does the governor offer with righteous indignation the social solutions of segregation and sterilization, he compounds the minority-group status of Pineys by recommending that non-Pineys enforce the exclusionary policies, or receive punishment themselves: "The decent folk of the district are to be pilloried if they do not see that the law is enforced against their worthless neighbors . . ." (New York Sun, June 29, 1913).

The depressed social conditions of the Pineys are noted by the governor, but in the scientific mode established by Goddard and Kite, he interprets the cause-effect relationship as one of genetic inferiority to poverty. He goes on to cite the poverty, the lack of education, since children go to work at "such a tender age," conditions that were prevalent in cities and rural areas alike in the dawn of twentieth-century industrialization; but they were conditions that would have required vast changes in the social and political organization of the country.

Social Class and Moral Codes:
The Piney Is Different

In his flamboyant, one-day motorcade through the Pinelands in 1913, the governor of New Jersey took note of the woods and forests, the tang and scent of the pines, and the blackened tree trunks that had been ravaged by fire, and concluded that it was not a fitting place for those who lived there: "It did not seem fitting that squalor, vice and sin should be found in so lovely, if mysterious a countryside" (New York Sun, June 29, 1913).

It was "sin and squalor," however, that were the real rationales for the Piney position of pariah. The governor was shocked to discover common-law marriages. Not equipped with the analytic vision of a social scientist, the observer is unable to place these informal arrangements, so common in isolated communities that exist outside the institutions of the larger society.

In the following passage, we have Governor Fiedler's observation and analysis of this issue:

> You stopped at a tumbledown clapboard house to find a woman and children bearing an old and distinguished name, but no man. The husband had gone to live with another woman who had left her own husband. The woman was thinking of letting another man live with her. . . . There was nothing about the mother to betray the generations of vicious living back of her except a curious look in the eyes, a gaze something like that of a wild animal. . . (New York Sun, June 29, 1913).

Goddard, Kite, and, later, Fiedler observed the patterns of common-law marriages in the Pine Barrens, a practice accepted and structured by the exigencies of rural isolation as it was by poorer classes in general; but since these patterns were not sanctioned in their own upper class structure (though they certainly did occur), the scientists linked such behavior with sin, and sin, in turn, with feeblemindedness.

It was a cruel injustice to the Pineys, whose greatest sin was they they were poor. As George Bernard Shaw was later to proclaim in his play-thesis on the social classes in England, Major Barbara, "poverty is the greatest sin of all." In Shaw's mold for the upper class Major Barbara, who joins the Salvation Army to rid the poor of their sins, Elizabeth Kite, an educated, upper class young woman, can only record the manifestations of poverty; she cannot interpret the social ramifications. Compare, for example, the description of the visit to the poorhouse in Dickens' David Copperfield with Kite's field notes on a visit to a branch of the Kallikaks whom she has tracked down to Brooklyn, where they had moved:

> In a back tenement, after passing through a narrow alley . . . after climbing a dark and narrow stairway, one came to a landing from which a view could be had of the interior of the apartment. In one room was a frowsled young woman in tawdry rags, her hair unkempt, her face streaked with black, while on the floor two dirty, half-naked children were rolling. . . . The field worker made her way as best she could across heaps of junk that cluttered the room . . . a hideous diseased cat was curled in the sunshine. . . (Goddard 1913:87).

It is at this point that Dickens and Kite separate in their interpretation of the cause and effect relationship. Dickens saw the legal structure and the institutions within the society as the responsible agents in the conditions of the poor. Kite, on the other hand, looks at the mother and decides that her cooperativeness in being interviewed is a clear sign of feeblemindedness. She writes of her willing subject: "She appeared to be criminalistic, or at least capable of developing along that line."

If people of the Pines had not been wary of government and bureaucracies before this time, they had certainly found just cause to close their doors to agencies and agents of the mass society. It is somewhat remarkable that they would share their cabins and food and songs with Herbert Halpert, who in the late 1930s roamed through the region collecting folk songs and legends of the Pine Barrens for what ultimately became his doctoral dissertation in literature.

Halpert notes that he found them reserved and quite suspicious of strangers—similar to the Jackson Whites in the Ramapos. The Jackson Whites, a racially mixed people residing in somewhat rural isolation in the New York-New Jersey border of the Ramapo Mountains, have been described as descendents of Revolutionary America similar to the Pineys, though little evidence has been developed in research to support this assumption. So, in a similar sense, they resembled the locals of the Arrow Lakes region in Canada, whose problems of displacement and resettlement were described by Wilson (1973). Here, too, as in the Pine Barrens, an isolated mountain region west of Calgary evolved a people and a life style that was both removed and mistrustful of the mass society, though not without some relevant experience in past history. Fortunately, Halpert was certainly not unaware of the effect of Kite's work on such attitudes. In an interview with Kite in 1940, some 27 years following the publication of the Goddard thesis, he quotes her as saying: "Anybody who lived in the Pines was a Piney. I think it was a most terrible calamity that the newspaper publicity took the term and gave it the degenerate sting. . ." (Halpert 1947:12).

Although Kite was still unwilling to accept the responsibility for her part in the stigmatization of the Piney, she did, at least by 1940, acknowledge the role that the environment had contributed to the human ecology and life style in the Pines: ". . . poverty in the Pines came from the acid soil which does not adapt itself to ordinary agricultural pursuits. When the industries died down, the people couldn't make a living. These people made a living by picking the wild berries and moss for florists" (Halpert 1947:12).

The stigma of the Piney was hard to die, however. The sharp antagonism between the people of the woods and those in the small towns bordering the area was recorded (Halpert 1947). There was also friction between the Pineys and the "country" people, as the neighboring farming populations were called.

In summary, then, the life style of the Pineys, living as they did in harmony with nature, as hunters and gatherers, as people who seldom complained to this author of being poor "as long as there's food to eat," helped to keep them removed from the political and social institutions of the mass society. This system of human ecology, coupled with the negative benefits of the stigmatization, kept the Piney outside organizations that lobby for land use decisions. They are, from their own description, frightened and timid and certainly mistrustful of outsiders.

The following description of a Piney came from an interview with a Piney, Gladys Eayre. She makes her living as part of a folk singing group, the Pine Coners, though she describes her youth as living in the woods and learning to hunt with her father and brothers. Gladys defines a Piney this way:

48 / ENVIRONMENTAL DECISION MAKING

> [Pineys?] that's us. You've heard of stump jumpers?
> It's just a widgeon that's the only thing I know of.
> Some people say you can't call them that because they
> get angry. They don't like to be called that, but that's
> what they are. Back in Chatsworth we call them
> "Widgeons." Oh yeah, that's a little creature—very
> frightened, timid—they'll peek at you from behind a
> tree; they don't like you they don't know you, forget
> it. You might as well get out when you can.

The following story that she related depicts the fate of a salesman who wanders too far back in the Pines and is encouraged to get out when he can:

> It's not that bad now. Used to be. I went back there
> with J.'s uncle. They knew us so they let us in. But
> some kind of a salesman got lost and he wanted to know
> if he could call and find out where he's supposed to work
> and while he was calling they stripped his car, and he
> came in and wanted to know where the police was, and
> they says go down the road a mile and you'll find it.
> There's nothing down there a mile so when he came
> back there was no trace of his car and the state police
> was there and took him away. . . .
> They had their own stills and their own venison
> market and you don't let strangers come in when you
> got things like that. Yeah, this was great for stills
> around here [about 35 years ago]. There was one not
> far from where we are now—biggest producer. Feds
> had a hell of a time finding him, but they did.

Isolation in the woods and forests was a part of the Piney self-concept, a source of pride and even humor. The following folk tale illustrates this point:

> Woman down clost to Tuckerton lived back in the
> woods. And the preacher went there one day to see
> 'em. And he says, "Lady don't you know that Christ
> died?" She says, "I told John the other day, livin'
> way back in the woods, hardly ever get a newspaper,
> that we don't know what's goin' on" (Halpert 1947:404).

Some stories and legends dealt with the supernatural, magic and witchcraft, the devil and his spirits. The continuity of folk songs, the themes of folk legends and tales serve as indicators of a culture held together through isolation, where a hunting and gathering and small-scale subsistence agriculture system prevails, and where the outside society can only threaten or exploit this way of life.

On the other hand, the devil legends, and more specifically the Leeds Devil or Jersey Devil, are discussed with equally somber tones, as they might have been told in the seventeenth century. For example, while driving through the woods with a college-educated local Pine Barrens resident, he stops the car to announce that this very spot is where the Jersey Devil lives. I smile. He in turn warns that this is not a joke, but to be taken most seriously—the Jersey Devil exists!

In 1975 a Sierra Club hiking leader decided to schedule a hike through the Pine Barrens, and, for added drama, he announced in the bulletin that the hike would include a search for the Jersey Devil. Somehow it was picked up in a local newspaper and the story was carried that the Sierra Club hike was looking for the Jersey Devil. Shortly thereafter, the hiking leader received several phone calls from persons quite seriously advising him on how to catch the devil.

The persistence of these early American folk legends, particularly the devil and fiddle folklore, serves as a signpost for the isolation, the contained culture, and the relative absence of industrial America, that is, until the beginning of the 1960s, a turn of events that is discussed in the next chapter.

Pineys as Nonparticipants in the Planning Drama

For all the factors mentioned in this chapter—the stigmatizing effect of social Darwinism, the life style that harmonizes with the natural environment, the geographic separation fostered by miles of woods and sandy roads that seem to go nowhere (and, in some cases, they do)—the Pineys have remained outside the political and social system that dictates local power structures. Although a small group of Pine Coners have become visible in recent years, their visibility is more in terms of preserving their culture than in actual participation in the power struggle. While the Pine Coners have generated a Piney consciousness, and even circulated a "Piney Power" button, their traditional mistrust of government and institutions of the larger society have left them outside of planning groups and environmental decision making in general. In recent months, the paths of environmental activists and the Pine Coners have passed via the increasing number of conferences held on the Pine Barrens within the state. Environmentalists and researchers consider the musical group environmental supporters; but the group of folk musicians expresses some uncertainty as to how they fit in all of the political machinations of the process of environmental decision making. As a result, Pineys in this book are distinguished by their nonparticipation.

By contrast, the second group of people of the Pines, the farmers and small businessmen, are the dominant political group in the region. Their role in environmental decision making has been major and significant in terms of development versus preservation policies.

FARMERS AND SMALL BUSINESSMEN: POLITICS AND PUBLIC PARTICIPATION

The Pine Barrens did not produce a great industrialist nor, as may be expected, a great industry. While the Pineys living back in the woods maintained a preindustrial, rural, subsistence level of farming and hunting and gathering, the people of the towns were engaged in a multiple system of fishing, clamming, farming, and, in very few cases, small businesses.

The closer they settled along the Delaware Bay, or the Atlantic Ocean, the more they engaged in shipbuilding and fishing. Their activities were not greatly varied from the Pineys, except that they lived in or nearer to villages, prided themselves that they had churches and schools, and were more prosperous because of their access to the bay or to land ownership.

Many of the families of the townspeople and farmers have been there for generations, descended from the early Quakers, with names that might have been taken from one of Hawthorne's novels: Leeds, Leek, Cranmore (and several variations such as Cranmer and Cramer), Haines, Alloway, and Thompson.

The Farming Community and the Politics of Land Use

Farming activity in the Pine Barrens is almost exclusively cranberry and blueberry growing, as the soil, highly acid in composition and sandy in texture, is fit for few other crops. Many of the more than 50 cranberry growers in the state are blueberry farmers as well; and of those 50, only four are independents while more than 90 percent are members of the giant farm cooperative. The Ocean Spray national farm co-op is a Hanson, Massachusetts, farm cooperative that processes 60 percent of the annual U.S. cranberry crop into sauce, juice, and other products.

Rapidly accelerating in growth patterns, the co-op recently amended its charter and bought a grapefruit processor and succeeded in organizing the Florida citrus growers into a cooperative pool to supply the plant. Therefore, while the wooded landscape of the Pine Barrens may suggest an isolated, rural setting, the institutional arrangements for the marketing of the crop is a major national industry. Appropriately, the leadership strata of Pine Barrens farmers and businessmen are hardly "dirt farmers." They attend national farm conventions and are elected to the boards of national and state collective organizations.

Those who play the role of spokespersons for the region are all college educated, at least one generation removed, with professional degrees and even occupations that enlarge their base as agriculturists. Because they are more articulate and politically connected to the agricultural and political party networks, the sphere of influence reaches well beyond the local political structure. More importantly, leaders of the broadly based farming community (which includes businessmen, trailer camp owners, developers, and landholders in general) are themselves the major landholders of the region, acquiring land through generations of inheritance and later through acquisition of parcels left dormant from the time of the Depression. They speak for and act as the protector of the average, smaller farmer who may have less education or interest in politics in general. One of the independent growers opposed to the preponderant influence of co-op leaders commented on this phenomenon critically: ". . . most farmers don't like to speak; they say, 'Oh, let so and so do that.' They feel they're not informed. Local people don't want to get involved." The result of this set of attitudes is that very few large landholders have become the major spokespersons and political activists for the entire farming community and even for the region. Significantly, this particular leadership forcefully opposes government management or control of land and water resources in the Pine Barrens, and their power to effect these decisions is enhanced by the attaining of numerous appointed or elected positions on land and water planning or regulatory commissions. Planning groups themselves are comprised of developers, builders, local mayors, and old-line conservationists who endorse the ideology of localism and populism, if not laissez faire land management policies; and the rallying point for the constituency is the old populist ideology of independence, autonomy, and fear of state or federal takeover. Thus, a local supporter of government management of the resources reports the following dialogue with an opponent, who was also a recent college graduate: "He said to me, 'This is the frontier—you fight your own battles.' But I tried to explain to him that the frontier is over. . . ."

The core beliefs in the old rugged individualist and frontier independence blend remarkably well, with the effects on a separate level of big business. Consensus is achieved through a strong system of in-group, out-group labeling, and the system is effective. Commented one cranberry grower wryly: "When you're from somewhere else, no matter how long you live here, you're from somewhere else."

The in-group, out-group labeling is selectively applied. Those who support the "home rule" position are referred to as a "good guy" or a "good old boy," regardless of how long the family has lived in the Pines. For example, some growers and businessmen are of more recent vintage than the old Quaker heritage. Some are descended from the immigrant Italian fruit pickers who, at the turn of the century, were rounded up each year in Philadelphia and settled in the Pine Barrens as seasonal workers. Even fewer married Quaker descendents and remained to become landholders. While some two-thirds of the cranberry farmers in the region are from original Pine Barrens families, others migrated southward from Trenton only 10 or 15 years ago.

Consensus determines whether the label of outsider applies to a given individual. One who opposes the dominant position on a land use decision is often reminded that he is an outsider, that he came from somewhere else. Thus, one such man was told: "I was about to say back during your father's time, but I can't say that to you cause your father wasn't living here." Nor is it unusual that someone at a public meeting will state that they are probably the only Piney in the room, suggesting that their roots in the region are proportionate with their right to dictate resource policy. Therefore, the stated reason for social and political cohesion on the local level is historical—origins and roots—no matter how poor the goodness of fit for that notion. On the other hand, critics of local-control leadership refer to those individuals as "tired cranberry growers," a term that means that the man is ready to get out of farming.

If there are tired cranberry growers, the winter of their discontent would have begun around 1959, when a chemical innovation in farming inadvertently produced an economic crisis for the large-scale grower and the virtual disappearance of the small-scale farm.

The Decline of Agriculture on a Small Scale

When a chemical weed killer, aminotriazole, was distributed as a sample to the various cranberry-growing states of New Jersey, Massachusetts, Wisconsin, and Oregon in 1959, it was viewed as a possible boon to the endless problem of weed control. Just before Thanksgiving of that final year of the 1950s, however, the U.S. public was told that this year's cranberries were contaminated with a chemical weed killer known to cause cancer in animals.

POPULATION & THE HUMAN ECOLOGY / 53

After that story was carried in the newspapers, one grower recalled: "That year [1959] you couldn't sell cranberries to your mother." Despite the fact that the chemical was reported to have been tested only in Oregon, it affected the cranberry operations throughout the Pine Barrens. One grower, Charles Thompson, asserts that it was never used in New Jersey; another remembers that his brother, who was then the expert in the family, had gone out and buried the sample—to this day they do not know where.

The industry was negatively affected for a solid three years before growers were to return to full production again. During that critical time period smaller and poorer farmers were forced to leave the land and to sell out to the larger owners, as this second group was able to obtain loans to hold out until the scare had passed over.

Other farmers have sold their land for different reasons. One older man had a severe case of arthritis and the constant work with near freezing water at cranberry harvesting time exacerbated his condition. In other families, the younger members seek a college education, become professionals, and have no interest in entering the family business. Thus, the long line of cranberry and blueberry farmers has been moving toward a decline in the number and succession of growers.

What is significant in this portrait of a changing economic system is that agriculture in the small Pine Barrens communities had reached a turning point in the early 1960s, a turning point that coincides with the eruption of land use conflicts discussed in the next chapter. Because these conflicts relate to the development of retirement communities, and to the appearance of newcomers to the once-stable population, this topic will be dealt with only briefly in this chapter.

THE NEWCOMERS: RETIREMENT VILLAGES AND SUBURBAN DEVELOPMENT

During the 1970s population growth, at least in Ocean County, has been the direct result of the construction of retirement communities. An estimated 40 to 50 percent of this county's growth from 1970 to 1976 was the result of senior citizen migration; and the spread of retirement villages into Burlington County has been in evidence.

To the planners and officials of the small Pine Barrens communities, the migration of this population is a boon to their limited economy, as retirement villages meet the problems inherent in a rural region in transition. Senior citizens are generally retired citizens and show limited concern for their placement in proximity

54 / ENVIRONMENTAL DECISION MAKING

to a center of employment, or to access by public transportation to metropolitan regions. Moreover, their presence does not usually include school-age children as part of the family unit, and they do not require the expansion of schools and other related facilities. Therefore, senior citizen housing seldom overloads the limited services in the communities on which they fringe, though they do require the expansion of hospital facilities and have begun to lobby in this direction.

Local municipalities and freeholders in general are responsive to the newcomers since they help to raise the tax base while voting against the expansion of schools, two concerns close to the hearts of local officials.

Mort Cooper's story on the jetport protest meeting in Toms River, discussed in the next chapter, illustrates the point that senior citizens from leisure villages have been recruited by local officials and even bussed to Trenton to form cheering sections during hearings on land use issues. For the time being, the people of retirement villages support the factions of localism and continue to increase their activity in the arena of public participation.

In summary, we have looked at three groups of people of the Pines: the Pineys, the farmers and small businessmen, and the newcomers in retirement villages. What we can see from this analysis of their role in environmental decision making is that three distinct categories of social and political participation are discernible: the nonparticipant, who is, of course, the Piney; the full participant, comprised of the old structure of local power; and finally, the marginal participants, the newcomers. It is hoped that this analysis uncovers the subtle distinctions between people living in the Pine Barrens, a complex arrangement often overlooked in the sweeping generalities that label all Pine Barrens residents as Pineys and all Pine Barrens locals as either developers or environmentalists. With this analysis presented, the following chapters that deal with changes and conflicts in the 1960s, and later in the 1970s and 1980s, are illuminated by this dimension of human ecology.

3

THE PINE BARRENS IN THE 1960S: CONFLICTS BETWEEN CONSERVATION AND DEVELOPMENT POLICIES

> Since the beginning of World War II, the American Society has been changing continuously. This change has been in direction as well as rate. The total amount of change has been so vast and radical that it can only be recognized as a social and cultural revolution.
>
> Bensman and Vidich 1971:5

New technology and automation generated by the requirements of war production during World War II and by postwar prosperity produced a long-range revolution in the U.S. society of the 1950s and 1960s. The four major causal factors of the "new society" were: tremendous increase in productivity due to automation; continuous growth of industrialization and the greater productivity of capital; increase in productivity achieved through the use of large-scale bureaucratically organized corporate giants; and emergence of a new middle class. In addition, the Keynesian solution of sustaining full production and employment in the U.S. economy laid the basis for large-scale expenditures by federal and state governments to stimulate and sustain the economy (Galbraith 1967; Bensman and Vidich 1971).

A further factor contributing to the economic growth of post-World War II society was the fact that in the two decades following, from 1947 to 1966, there had been no serious depression and only one year in which real income in the United States had failed to rise (Galbraith 1967).

Expanding industrialization and economic growth made possible the evolution of new suburban communities. Suburban growth represented one stage of urban decentralization, "occurring when there were still large tracts of undeveloped land relatively close to large cities and when there was also a substantial reservoir of nonmetropolitan areas . . ." (Fava 1975:12).

Ultimately, the ever-widening circles of urban and suburban development reached rural settlements. These areas were attractive to developers: They were low in population density, and therefore considered rural, but the larger economy was no longer small-scale and agricultural. Urban decentralization was occurring at the same time as the decline of older systems of agriculture, particularly in the highly urbanized regions of the northeast. In New Jersey, as well as Long Island and Massachusetts, the decline of the amount of land utilized for agriculture created opportunities for residential, commercial, and industrial development, and continued to enlarge the urban centers in their ever-widening ring.

SUBURBAN DEVELOPMENT AND AGRICULTURAL DECLINE

This urban decentralization and suburban development had its beginnings in the expanding society of the post-World War I period, when the crowding of urban slums and the need for construction of moderate-cost housing spurred the concepts of planned communities in density-controlled greenbelts in low-cost land close to rapid transit systems of cities (Stein 1957). The New Towns concept, originating with the English concern for urban crowding within cities, began at the turn of the century with the revolutionary pamphlet by Raymond Unwin, "Nothing Gained by Overcrowding" (Stein 1957:22) and found translation to U.S. conditions in the early 1920s. Sunnyside Gardens, Queens, the nearest point to Long Island, was constructed between 1924 and 1928 and utilized out-of-use farmland that had remained open space for some 35 years prior to acquisition. Significantly, during that "ripening" period, the cost of land rose from 3.3 cents per square foot in 1892 to 48.5 cents in 1910, which the City Housing Corporation paid the railroad for property held out of use for some 18 years.

Similarly, in 1928 Radburn was selected as a second New Towns site from a large tract of undeveloped fertile farmland in the Borough of Fairlawn, New Jersey, only 16 miles from New York. Residents of early suburbia were middle income, young, almost exclusively from New York or New Jersey and were commuters to New York City. Further development of suburbia was deferred by the Depression of the 1930s and World War II.

Post-World War II society saw the return to suburban housing development on a much larger scale and this time without the density control and greenbelt concepts of the earlier planned communities. Undeveloped farmland in central New Jersey became the site of a new Levittown where rural Willingboro had once existed. The urban expansion continued throughout the state of New Jersey until ultimately it reached its most isolated, undeveloped regions.

In summary, then, the concern for crowding in metropolitan and urban centers resulted in the development of suburban communities close to major cities and built upon vacant farmland, open space that had become available for nonfarming uses. Thus, urban decentralization was occurring at the same time as the decline of older systems of agriculture. It was only a question of time, then, before the Pine Barrens would respond to similar pressures.

THE PINE BARRENS AWAKES TO URBAN PRESSURES

The Pine Barrens region, at least visibly, remained untouched by urban decentralization and suburbia. It was still too far away, too limited in the development of transportation systems, not close enough to New York or Philadelphia to generate suburban development in the early 1960s. The northern New Jersey open spaces, closer to the New York metropolitan centers, were only beginning to reach saturation levels in suburban population growth, and the movement was progressing southward. Their distance from the metropole bought for the Pinelands "a gift of time," a decade more of "things moving very slowly" while northeastern New Jersey was galloping toward the anticipated and then desirable goal of full economic development.

Awareness of the existence of the Pine Barrens region and its marketability did not occur until the later 1960s. By the 1960s the abundant woodlands were regarded by many of the inhabitants as "leftovers" in the landscape. In the crucial years between 1960 and 1980, entrepreneurial developers were progressively working out new methods to link the continued post-World War II affluence of the evolving urban field with empty rural space.

The concept of the urban field (Friedmann 1973) is an attempt to define the relationship between the interconnecting systems of expanding cities and the once-isolated rural settlements. Thus Friedmann (p. 62) makes the point that "Farms and forests are interspersed with clustered urban settlements and centers of productive work. But the land is no longer primeval: in a fundamental way, whether its use is in agriculture or not, it has become 'urbanized.'"

This process of urbanization of agricultural regions is effected by the technologies of post-World War II United States, which make possible communication and regional transportation systems that extend beyond the traditional boundaries of rural or urban settings. Freidmann (p. 62) illustrates the concept with the following example: "Architects call it a 'plug-in-city,' by which they mean that anywhere within the urban field one can connect his home to an intricate and, for the most part, efficiently managed network of freeways, telephone, radio and television outlets and electric energy and water supply systems."

By this definition, the Pine Barrens existed within the urban field of two major urban regions. Though a rural, agricultural region, it was 40 miles from Philadelphia, 80 miles from New York City, and barely 30 miles from Atlantic City; but in the early 1960s the Pine Barrens had not yet become interconnected to the urban field.

Plans for development of a supersonic jetport in the remote Pine Barrens brought into focus the conflicting forces of conservation versus development for the first time in the history of the region. The plans to develop an intercontinental jetport served as a catalyst for the emergence of a wide variety of interest groups that raised new issues and the pressures on the area during the next two decades.

THE JETPORT CONTROVERSY

During a long and tortuous period of discussion and debate, plans to build an intercontinental jetport in the early 1960s encompassed at one time or another no less than 17 different suburban and rural settlements within the New York metropolitan region. In its course, the jetport controversy activated interest groups, community organizations in conflict with private industry, and governmental agencies over the use of the land. The conflict pitted for the first time citizen interest groups against the Port of New York Authority, industrial giants, and state government agencies. Certainly this was true for the Great Swamp controversy (to be discussed later in this chapter) in which affluent suburbanites pressured legislators to hold the line against penetration into their environs by the major urban, industrial sector in a conflict they defined as community preservation. The jetport controversy resulted in the formation of interest groups in New Jersey that ultimately (and after many transformations) became the parties in the land use conflicts in the Pine Barrens.

In the Pine Barrens, local government officials, the county freeholders, themselves initiated studies that would serve to convince the Federal Aviation Agency (FAA) that the region was ripe for development. The Board of Chosen Freeholders of Burlington County in the late 1950s had made numerous requests to the FAA to endorse its application to the Community Facilities Administration of the Housing and Home Finance Agency for an advance of $300,000 to aid in financing the cost of planning for the jetport. The 1961 Port of New York Authority planning document makes note of this local interest in economic development: "Thus, it is clear that the officials of Burlington County propose to develop one extremely large airport to serve the turbojet needs of the several large metropolitan areas along the East Coast and we have conducted our study of this problem on that concept." Within the Pinelands, local entrepreneurial factions represented by the county freeholders favored development linking the Pine Barrens to the industrial economy.

Chapter 5, "Cleavage and Organizational Strategy," deals with the late 1960s and early 1970s and analyzes a second generation of conflicts and interest-group formation. The issues focusing on the development of the Pinelands Environmental Council brings into center focus the emerging pattern of localism versus state and federal bureaucracies. Analysis in both issues—the jetport controversy and the Pinelands Environmental Council—concentrates on the social and political forces underlying conflicts between conservation and development policies. It was the jetport, however, that triggered the long line of conflicts that followed.

THE PLAN FOR THE JETPORT: THE PORT OF NEW YORK AUTHORITY

The Port of New York Authority had been operating the major commercial air terminals in the metropolitan area of northern New Jersey and New York since 1947, when the two states had entered into a statutory agreement that all of the metropolitan air terminals would serve the entire district. Coordinating and regionalizing the transportation systems was one indicator of the extent that the urban field cut across traditional state boundaries:

> The policy and determination of the two states, as declared in their 1947 statutes, to provide "proper and adequate air terminal facilities" for the benefit of the people of the states of New York and New Jersey and for the increase of their commerce and prosperity, pointed to the necessity for Port Authority studies of the problem of providing a new regional airport (Port of New York Authority 1961:1).

Commercial and cargo air transportation was viewed in the late 1950s and throughout the 1960s as an ever-expanding industry whose technological development could be attributed to the jet, which was, in turn, a product of intensive aeronautic design and production during World War II. Furthermore, intercontinental flights were the sole economic purview of the New York-New Jersey metropolitan region and, as such, were viewed as a major industry to be continuously expanded and developed.

David Goldberg, who was New Jersey Commissioner of Transportation during the administration of Governor Hughes in the 1960s, made the following observation to this author:

> . . . at that time, it was unheard of that intercontinental flight would be anywhere else in the country. It was the Gateway to Europe. In those days New York held a position it has since lost. You couldn't get a flight to Europe anywhere in the country except from New York. It gave New York an economic pre-eminence—they were fearful they could not service that traffic unless they do something. At that time they believed that the aviation industry would continue to grow and expand. . . .

The Port Authority report of May 1961 cites a three-year study of the region's economy developed by Harvard University for the Regional Plan Association and reports that "the Metropolitan Region will continue to grow despite decentralizing influences of the past two decades" (p. 4). The influences referred to were the westward shift in the U.S. population, wage-scale differentials, the high cost of space in the region, and the depletion of some types of skilled labor. However, it was anticipated that, given the hegemony of air cargo potentials and intercontinental flight within the metropolitan region, aviation would be two or three times more important within the next ten years, and therefore, given adequate facilities, "it [the aviation industry] will knit the commercial life of the Region into the world's economy" (Port of New York Authority 1961:24).

Delays and stacking, however, were already considered a problem for the Kennedy-Newark-LaGuardia airports. Given the expected exponential growth for the next decade, a report on preliminary studies by the Port of New York Authority (December 14, 1959) indicated an urgent need for an additional major airport to serve the metropolitan district, and the site suggested was the Great Swamp in Morris County, New Jersey.

In summary, then, the development of suburban communities in the "leftover" open spaces of New Jersey (and Long Island), on abandoned farmland or fertile undeveloped farmland, was the initial step in the changeover from agricultural communities bordering on urban regions to residential communities connected with the urban field. Though this changeover commenced with the post-World War I society with the planned New Towns and greenbelts of Radburn and Sunnyside Gardens, the broader thrust in suburban growth came with the post-World War II society. This change was generated in particular by the new federal subsidies in housing through the Federal Housing Authority (FHA) and in general by the continuous growth of industrialization.

Continuous economic growth generated an apparently ever-expanding industry within the New York-New Jersey metropolitan region as well as a housing industry in its suburbias; and, like the residential sprawl of suburbia, the expanding aviation industry made demands upon the existing open space close to that region.

The result of the Port Authority search for a site for an intercontinental airport, we anticipate, was a controversy among communities already situated in suburban regions to deflect the airport from their environs. Thus the jetport controversy was the basis for interest-group formation in New Jersey and ultimately set the stage for later land use conflicts in the Pine Barrens.

PRIMARY JETPORT SITE: THE GREAT SWAMP

In a New York Times Magazine article (February 12, 1967), drama critic Brooks Atkinson wrote an ecological and political analysis of the Great Swamp-jetport controversy entitled: "Great Swamp is Good for Nothing—But Life, Knowledge, Peace and Hope." He described the issue in the following terms:

> It is a natural masterpiece, only 30 miles west of Times Square. When the air is clear you can see the peak of the Empire State Building from the ridges of geological till that surround the swamp. The contrasts are dramatic. Thirty million people live in big and small houses in the surrounding terrain; automobiles and trucks choke the cement highways that sweep around the swamp; railroads by on both the north and the south. Great Swamp is so centrally located to business and industrial institutions that the Port Authority would like to tear it apart and make it into a jet airport. But for many thousands of years Great Swamp has retained its independence and preserves in the midst of megalopolis

a living patch—seven miles long and three miles wide—
of primitive America. Progress has stopped where
Great Swamp begins. In New Jersey the density of the
population is 833 people to a square mile. But no one
lives in the interior of Great Swamp. Even in 1967
some parts of it are impenetrable because of quick-
sand and thick vegetation (Atkinson 1967:33).

Introduced in Atkinson's discussion was a perspective of land values based upon the ecological and recreational necessity of preserving open space. This was an important shift in the appreciation of land based on the newly discovered value of wasteland. Atkinson pointed out: "There was a time, not more than half-century ago, when the word 'swamp' was the equivalent of 'waste' or 'danger.' Swamps occupied wasteland that most people thought should be developed into real estate. . . . But swamps are now regarded as essential links in the chain of life."

The people of the surrounding communities who had raised a total of $1.5 million to buy the 3,000 acres (which was ultimately turned over to the U.S. Fish and Wildlife Service to be managed as the Great Swamp National Wildlife Refuge) had as their basic motive not the wildlife per se but, according to Atkinson, "to spare the community the bedlam of an airport." Former Commissioner of Transportation David Goldberg concurred that the overt reaction of the community was related to the adverse impact on themselves or, rather, their property. Nevertheless, property owners—upper middle class suburbanites—became the first coalition of political interest groups to fight a powerful agency on what was labeled, in retrospect, an "environmental issue." This labeling of the Great Swamp controversy as an environmental issue in a historical sense was suggested by Goldberg:

The Port Authority underestimated their opposition
when they picked out a site like that. The Great Swamp
was no little garbage dump. It was one of the most
affluent suburban communities in New Jersey and they
knew how to fight. They must have raised a "war
chest" of some two hundred thousand dollars first
time around.

To Goldberg, the jetport controversy, particularly in the Great Swamp area, was a watershed of the 1960s, "marking a turning point in our attitudes toward institutions and growth itself and in terms of our own concept of development."

The Port Authority, at least since 1939, had been an agency so highly respected that it would be hard to imagine opposition to its plans. In the preceding decade, the Port Authority was an agency of prestige and influence: In the eyes of the public, it could do no wrong. With the jetport controversy, however, the superagency badly scarred this image. Notes Goldberg:

> When they spoke, important business and civic leaders listened. They developed a kind of arrogance that a high degree of success and very little criticism would produce in anyone. They had just presumed that when they picked out a site they would be permitted to develop that site. Such a classic fight. But in those days that kind of sophistication was rather rare, rather limited. This group was no black ghetto—as usual, the rich led the way, raised a lot of money and forced the Port Authority to do a reappraisal. In 1961, and in the classic Port Authority style, they looked at the problem again and concluded they were right after all.

Although the Port Authority reaffirmed its choice of the Great Swamp in Morris County, the new report did present a site evaluation of 17 areas selected from New York and New Jersey. Each of these sites were rural or suburban communities in upstate New York, Long Island, or New Jersey.

FINAL CHOICE FOR THE JETPORT SITE: ENTER THE PINE BARRENS

Sites 13 through 17 all fell within the two major Pine Barrens counties, Burlington and Ocean, and, if not directly within the Pinelands itself, as in Lebanon State Forest and McGuire Air Force Base, were close enough to have produced a major impact on the region and the ecosystem. In reality, the FAA did not view these sites as practical or feasible. They noted in their report that

> [Newark is] the only other large city which we anticipate will need an entirely new major airport in the forseeable future in the New York metropolitan area. In this event, however, we cannot conceive that the Burlington County area, located some 75 ground-miles away, could possibly be considered a logical or practical site for a major airport to serve metropolitan New York (Port of New York Authority 1961:153).

At this point, the push for the jetport in the Pine Barrens came from the county government in Burlington, more than from the state government or the Port Authority. The FAA conclusions in the 1961 report make the following comments with respect to sites 13-17:

> . . . the matter of developing a "Jet Age Global Terminal" in Burlington County, New Jersey, has been the subject of detailed studies by this Agency on numerous occasions over a period of at least the last four years. Our initial interest in this matter stemmed from a request from the Board of Chosen Freeholders of Burlington County . . . to finance the cost of planning this project. . . (FAA Report 1961:153).

Thus the FAA report concluded that its findings should serve to encourage the county constituents to develop their plans for civil airports in "more realistic terms."

Though the 1961 report did not recommend the Burlington or Ocean county sites, the suggestion of such feasibility, however remote, was sufficient to generate a reaction from the citizens of these counties. Lifelong conservationists, described later in this chapter, were to concentrate their already existing bird-watching and wildlife preservation groups into antijetport lobbying; but the interest-group formation to oppose the intercontinental jetport in the Pine Barrens was, at this point, outside the political structure. A more powerful political pressure was to overshadow the intervention of interest groups. The selection of the Pine Barrens as a site was the unintended consequence of election politics in the race for governor.

THE POLITICS OF LAND USE AND THE RACE FOR GOVERNOR

It was an election year in New Jersey in 1961. Senator Hillary of Morris County had passed a bill in the state legislature prohibiting the construction of a jetport in a series of named northern New Jersey counties, including Morris County, the site of the Great Swamp. The northern suburban lobby against the jetport had enlisted the actions of their legislators to prevent, once and for all, the industrial intrusion into their quiet communities. The Morris County (and to a lesser extent Hunterdon County) interest groups lived on estate-farms, each with corrals and pastures for their stables of horses. The simplicity of the New England-style farmhouses belies the presence of old-wealth upper class.

A Democrat, Meyner, was governor; and while the gubernatorial primaries were in swing, Senator Hillary induced Meyner to hold a public hearing on the bill to prevent the jetport—at which time Meyner vetoed the Hillary bill.

Nevertheless, Richard J. Hughes, Democratic candidate for governor, presented a campaign pledge that he would not support a jetport in Morris or Hunterdon counties, both wealthy, suburban, northwestern counties whose votes were traditionally Republican.

Later, in the gubernatorial campaign of 1965, still during the search period for a jetport site, Hughes, who was subsequently elected, was forced to renew and honor his campaign pledge made in the Democratic platform in 1961: "We renew our pledge to prevent the establishment of a jet airport in the Great Swamp of Morris County, Hunterdon County or in any other settled residential areas of the state" (New York Times, April 11, 1967).

The pledge of 1961 was given to offset a pledge against a jetport given by the Republican contender for governor. A New York Times article on the subject states: "The pledge was renewed in 1965 with only the Governor's casual acquiescence, in the remote chance that Republican Hunterdon could be persuaded to vote Democratic—which it could not" (New York Times, April 11, 1967).

At least in northern New Jersey, the Times confirms Transportation Commissioner Goldberg's assessment that it was the affluent who led the fight. Accompanied by Republican assemblymen and state senators from Hunterdon and Morris counties, and bearing placards that read: "Keep Goldberg Out of Soleberg" and "Richard Judas Hughes," the 1,000 demonstrators in front of the State House in Trenton were described in the following passage:

> Most of the demonstrators were well-dressed women in tailored, tweedy suits. Some of them managed to squeeze into the Governor's reception room this morning to give him thousands of antijetport petitions wrapped in funereal purple and black ribbons. One of the Governor's aides remarked as he gazed outside at the chanting demonstrators, many apparently from affluent, fox-hunting communities, "I wonder if they brought their hounds" (New York Times, April 1, 1967).

The opposition by suburban communities to the jetport was based on a belief that such industrial development would pollute the air and streams, create noise pollution, and disturb the rural character of both counties. However, the antiairport movement was not restricted to New Jersey.

The impact of the aerospace industry on the environment and the power of suburban communities to alter airport development had received some acknowledgment from federal officials. M. Cecil Mackey, (then) assistant secretary of transportation, informed the aerospace engineers at a speech that "American society was rebelling against the problems caused by the airplanes they build. . . . The demand for a livable environment was a new dimension for aviation" (New York Times, October 25, 1967). Mackey noted that "if the demand for a livable environment was not met on 'acceptable' terms, people would just say, 'sorry, we don't want airplanes around anymore, we don't want to travel that way.'"

As of April 1, 1967, the Transportation Department was required by law to consider the environmental impact of any actions it would plan. Mackey saw the citizen's insistence on less degradation of his environment as the single most outstanding characteristic of the society of the 1960s. While the formation of suburban interest groups occurred in reaction to industrial growth and the potential destruction of suburban boundaries, Mackey argued that it had come at a bad time for aircraft builders, airlines, airport planners, and others facing the stresses of explosive growth in air travel.

Therefore, the environmental conflict that gathered momentum in the 1960s, we hypothesize, drew from two value systems on a collision course throughout the decade: the first, a concept of ever-expanding economic growth activated through automation and technology, and made possible structurally through the complex bureaucratic systems in the business and government sector; and the second, the rise in political consciousness of the new middle and old upper classes with the means—political, financial, or otherwise—to protect and preserve their social environment. This financial point is discussed at length in the final chapter of this book, where we postulate that participation of social classes in environmental disputes has shifted downward since the turn of the century to include this range of interest groups. However, it was economic growth, an increased expansion, that was the stimulus for environmental conflicts.

ENVIRONMENTAL CONFLICTS AND
ECONOMIC EXPANSION

In the past, environmental disputes and value conflicts were submerged under the nearly universal agreement that economic growth and efficiency were desirable (Tribe et al. 1976). Once this basic tenet becomes questioned, a consensus is no longer possible. Technology has become a double-faced monster in the contemporary society. It is both the savior of the economy and the sinner against the environment.

Thomson (1976) raises this point in discussing the Tocks Island Dam controversy, a dispute over land and water planning that brought the forces of New Jersey, New York, and Pennsylvania into political conflict over the flooding of a natural area for the presumed purposes of damming the Delaware River to preclude an urban water supply. She states:

> In a country where labor was scarce, land and resources plentiful, and mobility and economic growth highly valued, technology was developed and used to a greater degree than elsewhere. It was only natural, when problems developed to attempt to find technical solutions. Surely it is easier to change technology than it is to change man's practises and institutions (Thomson 1976:37).

In changing the environment by filling in lakes to form runways, by adding noise and pollution to suburban communities and rural settlements, the Port of New York Authority was destroying open land by raising its market price and tying it in closer to the urban, industrial areas. Cost-benefit analyses based upon market values could and did present favorable rationales for jetports and for suburban land development to provide housing for the growing ranks of the new middle class.

In the jetport controversy in New Jersey, it was not so much the idea of economic growth that was in question, but the overall effect of that growth and the direction it was taking. Technology was the means. Commoner, in *The Closing Circle* (1971:76) identifies the new technologies developed since World War II as the causal factor in the environmental crisis:

> The over-all evidence seems clear. The chief reason for the environmental crisis that has engulfed the United States in recent years is the sweeping transformation of productive technology since World War II. The economy has grown enough to give the United States population about the same amount of basic goods, per capita, as it did in 1946. However, productive technologies with intense impacts on the environment have sideplaced less destructive ones. The environmental crisis is the inevitable result of this counter ecological pattern of growth.

In modern industrial societies, technological development usually upsets the balance between prevailing human settlements and economic structures. It results in uneven growth and a maldistribution of perceived benefits and ill-effects. While upper and middle class suburban communities may organize and politicize to deflect the impact of industrial growth, leaders of rural settlements outside the urban field may organize and politicize to bring about a long-awaited industrial development.

For the Pine Barrens, the interest in developing the jetport somewhere within the "useless swamplands of the Pines" came from the local county government, the freeholders who represented business interests searching for profits through an economic connection to the urban-industrial field as indicated by their bid for a jetport to the FAA.

The response of the business-government local network to the prospect of a jetport and the potential for economic development was sharply different from that of upstate suburban lobbyists in the Great Swamp region. A distinctly rural settlement until the 1960s, the Pine Barrens survived economically with a limited-crop agricultural system. The sandy, acid soil could support primarily the development of cranberry and blueberry growing. It was in fact the separation from the northern, upstate industrial economy that led local factions in South Jersey to propose seceding from the state as a means of bolstering their own economy, or at least capturing the interest of state government. Consequently, the idea of the jetport for the Pine Barrens had local support. Ironically, the industrial interests within the state focused upon the Pine Barrens as a prospective jetport by default. The political and financial powers of the northern suburban communities didn't want the jetport in their own residential areas. At the same time low-cost land was available, and the urban planners were willing to develop this empty space.

THE JETPORT AND RURAL SETTLEMENTS
IN THE PINE BARRENS

During a nearly ten-year period, the search for a feasible jetport site persisted in suburban and rural communities in New Jersey and New York State. Battles were fought on a community-by-community level. Those involved were not fighting for the environment in general, nor for the region or the state in which they lived, but rather for their community alone. One example of this community-control issue appears in a letter to the editor of the New York Times concerning the Shoreham, Long Island community opposition to Governor Rockefeller's choice of Calverton as the jetport site:

A March 17 editorial supports Governor Rockefeller's
choice of Calverton as the site for an international jetport. The editorial leaves out . . . the special character of the region and the disruption that can result if the
proposal is carried out. Yet the lovely farmlands,
woodlands, and beaches of eastern Long Island are
surely as worthy of protection as the swamplands of
New Jersey so vigorously, and I think rightly, defended
by the Times (New York Times, March 21, 1967).

The jetport issue hovered like an albatross over the heads of
political and industrial leaders of both New York and New Jersey.
In the abstract the leaders welcomed the prospect of regional economic gain, but wherever they selected a site, the community so
chosen would respond by intense political opposition—the promise
of economic growth could not be dismissed.

ECONOMIC INCENTIVES

The Port of New York Authority report of 1961 noted that
during construction phases, a daily average of 2,000 construction
workers would be employed, and the total payrolls might approxi-
mate $85 million. The report cites (p. 5) the Hammer & Company
Associate Report on the economic gain to regions with the acceptance of a jetport:

Regional effects would be principally felt in terms of
expanded job opportunities and income flows generated
by the new employment in primary aviation activities
on and off the airport site and "multipliers" growing
out of successive rounds of spending and respending
the new income brought to the region by the airport
activities.

The totals based on initial and multiplier jobs and incomes are
represented below.

	Total Jobs	Regional Income
Primary aviation employment	95,130	530,400
Local purchases of primary aviation industry	16,400	78,000
Sales to passengers travel service	23,050	109,500
Total	$134,580	$717,900

70 / ENVIRONMENTAL DECISION MAKING

It is not surprising that the promise of high economic gain would create pressure for the jetport in New Jersey, certainly from the large industrialists within the state, as indicated below.

On August 24, 1967, Governor Richard J. Hughes led a group of New Jersey citizens to Washington, D.C. for a meeting with Alan Boyd, secretary of transportation, to discuss "the crisis of inadequate jetport facilities" in the New York-New Jersey metropolitan areas. What followed was the creation of the Governor's Economic Evaluation Committee for an Intercontinental Jetport for New Jersey (October 31, 1967). This group of distinguished businessmen was chaired by J. Seward Johnson, vice-president of Johnson and Johnson, and included the presidents of Prudential Life Insurance of America, Campbell Soup Company, and the Jersey Central/New Jersey Power Light Companies. This list included the most powerful businessmen and industries in the state. Their 1967 report, "A Proposal for an Intercontinental Jetport and a System of General Aviation Facilities," stresses the significance of economic growth: "No economy stands still. If it does not move forward, it declines. A jetport in New Jersey will assure economic growth, economic vigor, and economic opportunity for our growing population" (A Proposal for an Intercontinental Jetport 1967:2). In this 1967 report, the governor's committee dismisses the northern New Jersey suburban sites in Hunterdon and Morris counties, where some of them resided, and selected instead the McGuire/Lakehurst site, which would extend eastward from the instrument runway of McGuire Air Force Base and would then settle within the long-forgotten Pine Barrens.

The Pine Barrens, which was considered by the FAA to be an unrealistic and altogether unworkable choice in 1961, became the choice site in 1967. The reasons for this shift center upon both local and state pressures for economic development and the fact that other areas had successfully resisted the benefits of economic expansion.

The local interests in the immediate economic benefits inherent in jetport development was the local county freeholders' (themselves businessmen) position on economic development of the region, especially as a means of lowering real estate taxes. An old-line conservationist opposed to the jetport, and who has subsequently become a county planner, reports the following conversation with a freeholder: ". . . the idea of a jetport—and the Ocean County Freeholder director saying—'well, the Pine Barrens are ugly—I'm always happy when I'm through 'em on my way back from Trenton. Besides, they're a fire hazard and what's wrong with getting a lot of ratables out of it.'"

INTEREST-GROUP FORMATION: OPPOSITION TO THE JETPORT

Those opposed to the jetport in the Pine Barrens were a group of conservation-oriented people quite different from the northern parts of suburban Morris and Hunterdon counties. This group sprang from a loosely knit association of lifelong conservationists, organized in 1957 as an advisory committee to aid the state in the botanical development of the then recent purchase of the Wharton Tract by the state. This group of old-line conservationists and naturalists predated the Earth Movement of the 1960s, though they were later to gain acceptance by that movement.

These conservationists were old Yankees. Some came from the old families of Philadelphia and had settled in one of the few planned, exclusive communities like Medford Lakes. The single-family dwellings in this tree-lined lake district carved from a former cranberry bog are surrounded by abundant woodland and are far removed from the "little boxes" of the middle income Levittowners.

Dot Evert, member and leader of this group, describes the composition and selection of fellow conservationists: "The background of the people we picked were working in the Pine Barrens just for the love of it . . . photographing, studying—botanists and naturalists. Well we picked up a historian or two, and that been a very loose structured thing and still is. . . ."

These conservationists involved in lobbying against the jetport in the early 1960s were a highly select group of upper class and upper middle class persons with specialized leisure activities or professions that connected their interests to the continuance of the natural state of the Pine Barrens. Elmer Rawley, later chairman of the Audubon Society in the region, also lives in the Medford Lakes district in a wooded setting on the lake. In the tradition of upper class Yankee stock, he was a high-ranking officer in the military, and, following retirement, spends his frequent vacations, like the Everts, as a roving naturalist, often scuba diving off remote barrier reefs. High-ranking military and retired military are not uncommon to the Medford Pine Barren communities. They are an outgrowth of the military communities in nearby Fort Dix and McGuire Air Force Base whose ranking officers buy homes in the Pine Barrens and tend to remain there after retirement.

This group of old-line conservationists were not the "new middle class," described by Bensman and Vidich (1971). Their presence in the region may not be traced to the early Quaker settlers, as can some of the cranberry-growing families, but to the leisure activities of the "old wealth," a highly select and relatively small group of conservationists and naturalists of old urban wealth similar to those who had supported the conservation policies of Roosevelt and Pinchot at the turn of the century. Unlike the old urban wealth who concerned themselves primarily with preserving the remote Western lands, these conservationists resided in or near the Pine Barrens and saw the push for industrialization as an issue of land conservation and community preservation. They considered their conservation interests as being a minority position with respect to most other people in the state. Dot Evert made the following observation about changes in attitudes since the 1950s:

> We've come from the period of the 1950s when they looked on us as absolute dirt, really—most people and most intelligent people too thought there was nothing but a pine and oak mess till they got to the shore. But then in the 1960s, the young ones started to the Earth Movement and we had young ones coming to find out about the Pine Barrens. Always, from the very beginning, there have been interested people from every part of the world, as soon as they would get to Philadelphia, Dr. B or somebody would call and say "Dr. so and so is here, would you show him this or that?" So people have been interested since the Revolutionary days.

The jetport issue focused attention on the Pine Barrens to others outside this group of old-line conservationists. Not only were they engaged in interest-group formation to resist the recommendations of the Governor's Committee, they were the target of other communities that had been chosen as a possible jetport site. Recalls one conservationist, the struggle against the jetport was fought on a community-by-community basis in which one could attempt to deflect the development to the other:

> A lot of the pressure for the jetport in the Pine Barrens came from the Great Swamp people—they didn't want it there—and that was true of the Long Island people too. They were all for having the jetport in the Pine Barrens. . . . You'd open up the Times and you'd see that someone in Long Island said the Pine Barrens is the ideal place 'cause it's halfway between Philadelphia and New York. Ridiculous thing about that whole movement was that the airlines weren't for it at all.

THE MILITARY AS AN INTEREST GROUP

Not only were the airline companies cool to the idea of a Pine Barrens jetport site, but the military, particularly the air force, was resistant to giving up its base for civilian activity. The military bases formed a considerable portion of the Pine Barrens region: Fort Dix, McGuire Air Force Base, and the Lakehurst Naval Station. Therefore, a third interest group was the military complex, and the military resisted the move to transfer land they owned back to the state to provide the land for the jetport. Ownership of the Pine Barrens by the military is considerable and almost impossible to measure since farms and even towns such as Wrightstown bordering on the 55 square miles of Fort Dix are actually owned by the army.

The governor and some business supporters of the Pine Barrens site made futile trips to Washington to try to convince the military to yield the site to the state. Concurrently, the military was extending its activities into the Barrens and making its technological impact upon the ecology of the natural area. The National Guard proposed a tank training ground in the Pinelands.

The Citizens Committee to Save State Land, a group formed by the same Pine Barrens conservationists of FOCUS (Federation of Conservationists United Societies, Inc.) moved into action in 1964 to oppose this expansion. Together with the New Jersey Audubon Society, they saw to it that the governor's office was swamped with letters and telegrams opposing this military advance. They were also to enlist the help of the newly emerging Earth Movement. A member of the Citizens Committee recalls the success in the 1960s of letter-writing campaigns against the tank training program:

> . . . in the 1960s when the young ones started with the Earth Movement all we had to do was use the telephone service to stop this tank training program. The state man said they carried the letters into the governor's office in bushel baskets—just an overwhelming support from the public in the 1960s.

It is significant that the appeal to stop the military expansion went to the same governor whom the conservationists had opposed on the jetport expansion. In this case, however, it was an alignment of state structure and citizen interest groups against the federal military agency.

The emerging pattern of interest-group formation in the Pine Barrens centers on opposing positions on conservation versus development. The lines of conflicting views are suggested in the following paradigm:

FOR CONSERVATION	FOR DEVELOPMENT
<u>Old-line conservationists</u>	<u>Industrialists</u>
Pine Barrens conservationists	Johnson & Johnson
FOCUS: Ocean Nature and Conservation Society	Campbell Soup Prudential Life
	<u>State government</u>
Long Beach Island Conservation Society	Governor Commissioner of Transportation
Audubon Society of New York	
	<u>Local government</u> (also local businessmen)
	Burlington and Ocean County freeholders

<u>Military</u> (for and against specific development)

Fort Dix
McGuire Air Force Base

 The emerging positions on land use planning in the Pine Barrens fell sharply between conservation and development, with the exception of the military. The military groups fell somewhere in between. They opposed political control by the state and, though they may not have favored industrial development to the region, they wanted to pursue military development of the area.
 These interests in planning policy shifted in the late 1960s, the second era, and are presented in Chapter 5, when a merger of conservation interest groups with local business, government, and agricultural groups resulted in the regional planning body, the Pinelands Environmental Council. This planning body was formed from the real and "imagined" concerns for urban decentralization that emerged in issues raised over the development of the jetport. The receding of the jetport as an issue was ironically a product of technological impracticality and the subsequent lack of support from the largest agencies necessary to support its development. The airlines, the military, and the Port of New York Authority all rejected the Governor's Committee choice of the Pine Barrens as a feasible site.
 For the first group, the potential flight patterns would conflict with those of the Philadelphia Airport. The jetport plan for the Pine Barrens was as much defeated by the impracticality of the

location as anything else. Former Transportation Commissioner Goldberg contends that the major reason for the jetport was to service the metropolitan region, New York City, and northern New Jersey, but land travel time was too great for the Pine Barrens to have ever been a feasible site.

The 1961 Port Authority report would confirm this concern for the overland travel time and distance. For each of the 17 sites suggested, the report estimates the travel time and public transit service necessary to reach a key metropolitan area. For example, the Lebanon State Forest site would require almost two hours of land travel to reach downtown Newark, while the Great Swamp area was 25 minutes away from that same point.

Despite the land travel problems associated with the Pine Barrens site, the strong community opposition from both Morris County on the Great Swamp and Hunterdon County over the Soleberg Airport increased the feasibility of the Pine Barrens site, and as other alternative sites were eliminated because of local opposition, the search continued.

A final function that the jetport controversy provided was the rhetoric and symbols for local movements opposed to governmental management and intervention by locally based interest groups, which will be discussed in Chapter 5.

The final political move against the jetport came during still another race for the governorship in New Jersey in 1969.

THE RACE FOR GOVERNOR AND PINELANDS POLITICS: 1969-70

Small New Jersey communities, particularly in southern New Jersey, support political positions that favor decentralization of power, a concept often referred to as "home rule," and in general tend to vote Republican. The following report of public policy formation based on a political race serves to demonstrate the importance of land planning disputes in political campaigns. The report was given by an old-line conservationist who supports the Republican ideology of home rule and reflects his concern for decentralized power as much as it reveals candidate William Cahill's responsiveness to Republican constituencies.

Just before the time when the then Congressman Cahill was nominated as the Republican candidate for governor, a report requested by Governor Hughes, the Blomquist Report, had concluded that the jetport could be appropriately placed in the Pine Barrens. Led by the coalition of conservationists known as FOCUS, a mass meeting was called to discuss the jetport and the Pine Barrens.

76 / ENVIRONMENTAL DECISION MAKING

The conservationist recalls the day of the meeting in the following passage:

> . . . it was held at the Armory here at Toms River in February, and I recall very well there was 18 inches of snow the night before and the Armory is a little bit off the beaten track . . . and this mass meeting was set for a Thursday afternoon, I think, at 2:00 o'clock. . . .

The midday timing of the meeting made attendance possible for a large number of senior citizens from nearby leisure communities who were opposed to airport development:

> . . . and that's a working day during the week and yet they were able to put about 900 people in that Armory—very largely senior citizens from the senior citizens development . . . they were against the jetport too, 'cause they had come down here to retire . . . spent their whole life working for a living and kids are married and gone and they all come down to these senior citizen developments where they don't have to shovel snow and rake leaves and its all done for them—and right away you want to put a jetport alongside them so you hear all this beautiful noise like you do at Idlewild—what's that called now—Kennedy.

The response of senior citizens at the Toms River mass meeting was to oppose the jetport. They demonstrated and, in addition, enhanced political awareness by contacting the gubernatorial candidates about their concerns. Thus, the old-line conservationist reports the following exchange:

> . . . so when it ended up with this mass meeting over here, and after the speakers were finished, Ben Maybry, who was acting as master of ceremonies, said: "Well now, does anybody have any comments from the floor?" and a little old hand went up in the back and she said, "I'm secretary of the National Association of Retired Persons at Forked River and I wrote Congressman Cahill to get his opinion on this jetport controversy since he's running for office." And then Ben Maybry said, "Would you like to read the letter?" The first sentence from Cahill's letter said, "I've always advocated using McGuire Air Force Base as the supersonic jetport."

Embarrassed by the report of the projetport position by a Republican candidate, Maybry assumed that the congressman had been misquoted and requested that the letter be brought to the podium for careful examination. Indeed, according to the letter it was Cahill's position that a jetport at McGuire Air Force Base would be the best solution to the jetport problem. That position was to shift dramatically within 48 hours after local reports of the meeting had suggested that Cahill had committed political suicide with his projetport stance. His change of policy is recalled in the following commentary:

> That meeting was over about four o'clock in the afternoon and 20 minutes later I was back home and turned on the local radio station and the local station said, "Congressman Cahill may have committed political suicide this afternoon," and then they went on to describe this thing. Well within 48 hours, Congressman Cahill's platform had a plank put into it: no jetport anywhere in New Jersey.

Thus, in the race for governor, the Republican candidate Cahill shifted his position on the jetport possibilities in the Pinelands based on an "embarrassing" letter written to the secretary of a senior citizens interest group. Within 48 hours after his position was made public, the candidate changed from a pro- to an antijetport position.

The formation of public policy on land use planning was manifest most dramatically during election years when, in the 1960s and after, suburban and exurban communities were organizing pressures against urban decentralization via urban encroachment on rural areas. For example, over a nearly two-decade period, from 1960 to 1980, policies toward decentralization of urban regions were significantly changed during election years. Table 4 illustrates this point when we trace a shift in land use policies from prodevelopment in 1960 to the creation of land preservation commissions in 1977 by Governor Byrne.

The shift in the governors' policies toward the open-space areas within this highly industrialized state reflects the impact of citizen-based interest groups whose development into formal organizations resulted in a shift in power over planning toward the increasing suburban population of the state during the 1960s.

By 1967, because of local network lobbying, the governor of New Jersey appointed the Pinelands Environmental Council, a locally based group whose representation was designed to reflect agricultural, business, and rural political groups. The council

78 / ENVIRONMENTAL DECISION MAKING

was charged with the responsibility of planning for the preservation of the Pinelands. The outcome of this organization is discussed in Chapter 5. What was significant to these decisions was that planning responsibility was relegated to presumed citizen interest groups, as opposed to professional planners. In 1977, in the wake of the then waning Pinelands Environmental Council, Governor Byrne appointed a state-level Pinelands Review Committee, whose responsibilities were to delineate boundaries of the region and secure plans to preserve it. This shift in planning policies reflected the pressure and power generated by formally organized interest groups on environmental issues in the 1970s.

TABLE 4

Land Use Policies Drafted during
Election Years, 1960-77

Campaign Years	Governor	Political Party	Policy
1960-61	Hughes	Democrat	Campaign pledge: no jetport for Morris or Hunterdon County.
1964-65	Hughes	Democrat	Renews 1960 pledge. Considers Pine Barrens for jetport development.
1967-68	Cahill	Republican	No jetport anywhere in New Jersey. Establishes a Pineland Environmental Council, a locally based planning body.
1977-78	Byrne	Democrat	Save the Pinelands Policy Drafts Executive Order No. 56 to establish the Pinelands Review Committee—a state-level planning body.

Source: Compiled by the author.

Since these groups have become more organized, their differences over policy concerning conservation or development have escalated the conflict over planning rights and policies. These conflicts have, in turn, spurred the drafting of legislation by congressmen toward the financing and management of the Pine Barrens. These new forms of legislation are discussed further in Chapter 6, but it is important to note the changes in land use planning policies over the earlier two-decade period.

In the early 1960s the Pine Barrens was a forgotten region. Even when business-oriented county freeholders proposed a plan to build an intercontinental jetport in the Pines, the idea was treated with some scepticism by the FAA, which was more concerned with northern New Jersey suburban communities. The Pine Barrens was still too far away. Rather, preferred sites to extend the urban field were located closer to the metropolitan region. The organization of citizen interest groups in the northern locations forced consideration of the Pinelands by default. The creation of a citizen-based planning group, the Pinelands Environmental Council, by Republican Governor Cahill brought new conflicts, since many members of the council, including the chairman, were considered development oriented. The subsequent creation of the Pinelands Review Committee by Governor Byrne reached new levels of conflict since the forces of development versus preservation have subsequently organized, intensified their political actions, and, finally, splintered across group lines.

SUMMARY

As an environmental issue, the jetport receded from the Pine Barrens for a complex of reasons. Significantly, the organization of citizens and their attempts at influencing public policy on the question of open space had not occurred before the jetport controversy. This controversy created and transformed new interest groups and gathered together coalitions who would later be forced to regroup and redefine their goals and engage in active political efforts to influence state and federal bureaucracies, a process that is continuous and even more pluralistic in the 1970s and 1980s.

The increase in productivity due to automation, the growth of affluence, and the further urban decentralization, plus the greater productivity of capital that followed the post-World War II society, did not in itself generate visible change <u>within</u> the Pine Barrens so much as it created pressures in the more affluent and densely populated regions, which, in turn, affected rural settlements.

The Keynesian solution of sustaining full production and employment of the 1950s and 1960s meant that growth would include geographic changes, alter the use of land, and threaten undeveloped natural areas near urban settlements.

The decisions made by the Port Authority and industrial leaders and subsequent upper and middle class citizen interest groups could have had more far-reaching effects upon the Pine Barrens than in all of its previous 300-year history. Swamplands, pinelands, and wetlands were suddenly the center of political and social conflicts. Their interim resolution was in legislatively enacting land management policies that were to be carried out by state and federal agencies. Though this form of conflict settlement may have been part of Western land disputes early in this century, such political battles over conservation and preservation had not reached the industrial East Coast until the 1960s.

In the next phase of social and political conflicts, those of the late 1960s and mid-1970s, a second generation of problems and political alignments grew out of the initial struggle over conservation and development. How this drama is acted out must be understood within the analysis of interest-group politics and with knowledge of the vital role played by land and water both as resources and as the focus of conflict.

4

WATER AND LAND: CRANBERRIES AND HOUSING

> What we call land is an element of nature inextricably interwoven with man's institutions.
>
> Polanyi 1944:178

The lack of industrial growth in southern New Jersey, particularly in the Pine Barrens, was not, as we have indicated, the result of rational planning and decision making but rather a by-product of the limits of what the land could support.

THE UNION OF LAND AND WATER: CRANBERRY GROWING

The primary source of economic development in the Pine Barrens was agriculture, but there were and still are severe limitations on the varieties of crops possible on a soil so highly acid in composition. Primarily cranberries and blueberries can be grown. Moreover, water, especially an easily regulated water supply, was a readily available resource that cranberries require. The farmer could "capture" water in the bogs and use it as required during the cranberry growing cycle. To this end, each grower actively worked to attain control of a stream, as a basis for dams and streams, reservoirs, canals, ditches, along with pipes, wells, and overhead sprinklers (Thompson 1974).

Flooding plays a dual role in the growing and harvesting of cranberries. Cranberry vines are shallow and subject to damage when a heavy freeze gets into the ground. To avoid this hazard, each grower must provide a "winter flood" starting about Christmas.

Hopefully, all vines are covered with water by the first week of January (Thompson 1974).

The flood remains on the vines until March, April, or May. While the water is on, the vines are dormant. If the water gets too warm, the start of the decaying process produces a scum in the water that may coat the vines. Where the winters are extremely cold, an ice cover on a bog may shut out light and oxygen so that the water's oxygen content drops. In this case, the vines may die from lack of oxygen. To discourage frost, growers use water in winter, but once spring produces higher temperatures, the water is removed and the vines begin to grow. Should a frost reappear in the spring, the bogs are reflooded. This flooding and draining serves to help maintain a bog temperature above freezing.

The second vital role of water is in the actual harvesting of cranberries. "Wet picking" harvesting requires that the bog be flooded while machines are utilized to "knock" or drag the berries from the vines into the water, whose depth is just over the vines. The hollow berries float on the surface of the water and are then skimmed from the water in hinged board enclosures. Once this is done, the water is passed on to the next bog and the process continued until all the berries have been harvested.

The "wet picking" method of harvesting is a relatively recent innovation and has reduced the necessity of migrant laborers. One cranberry farmer commented that in his grandfather's time, berries were hand picked and required hundreds of migrant workers, who for the most part were Philadelphia-based Italian immigrants. Their families had to be housed by the farmers and returned to the city after the harvest was completed. In his father's time, with the improved scoop methods of harvesting, a farmer required 50 to 60 workers and later on, only a dozen. With the present technology—machines and wet picking—the farmer requires only one part-time helper.

Since water as a resource was (and is) essential to growing cranberries, the early farmers bought up the vacant woodlands upstream so they could control the use and quality of water for their bogs. The result was that they became the major landholders of the region, although a very small portion of the land they owned was actually used to grow cranberry vines. Those who were marginal—were too far from a water supply—eventually went out of business and sold out to the larger landholders. The cranberry business became dominated by a few families who handed it down generationally. These families credit themselves with the preservation of the Pine Barrens since it was they who preserved the woodlands in order to maintain their water supply.

In a report of the Pinelands Advisory Committee presented to the freeholders of Burlington and Ocean counties in 1970, the committee comments:

> Water, the Pinelands most valuable resource, caused the growth and development of the most important industries in the area, the cultivation of blueberries and cranberries; water is the principal reason why so much of the Pinelands has remained virtually untouched by the ceaseless flow of modern civilization. . . . This vast territory [the Wharton tract] which remained in the Wharton family for generations along with the many thousands of acres owned by the cranberry and blueberry growers and used for the cultivation of their crops and for the protection of their water supplies was closed to adverse development, thus preserving the Pinelands in a largely natural condition. Municipal governments, dominated by gentlemen guided by traditional values, were not awed by the glitter of "progressive" innovations and did not encourage their establishment or growth.

It is water rather than the surrounding land that touched off the conflict between cranberry growers (and among individual cranberry growers) and state agencies since no one can, under state law, own the water resource, although one can own the land over and surrounding it. For cranberry growers, water is essential to crop growth and harvesting, but it is for other reasons of great interest to the state Department of Environmental Protection as a resource: It is a potential water supply to the entire state.

In a speech made by Rocco D. Ricci, then deputy commissioner of environmental protection, he raised the question of pluralistic participation in planning for the Pine Barrens and, more particularly, the surface water and ground water resources:

> What are the proper roles of the federal, state and local governments in Pine Barrens resource planning and management? What is the role of the public, the environmental groups and private citizens? However, we cannot wait until these complex interrelationships are worked out. We must act now. The DEP [Department of Environmental Protection] will be proposing within the next few weeks upgraded surface water quality standards and ground water standards including nondegradation provision for the waters of the Pine Barrens (Ricci 1976).

It is here that Ricci points out the potential resource of Pine Barrens water for the state: "The non-degradation of these unusually high quality waters is critical to maintaining the ecosystem and to their possible future use to provide for a broad range of water needs for the citizens of our state" [p. 3].

The ground water Ricci refers to is the aquifer, an underground water system equivalent to an enormous lake 2,000 square miles in area and averaging 37 feet deep.

John McPhee (1967:17) describes the magnitude and vulnerability of the ground water system:

> Typically, a pipe less than two inches in diameter driven thirty feet into the ground will produce 55 gallons a minute, and a twelve-inch pipe could bring up a million gallons a day. But, with all this, the vulnerability of the Pine Barrens aquifer is disturbing to contemplate. The water table is shallow in the pines, and the aquifer is extremely sensitive to contamination. The sand soil, which is so superior as a catcher of rain, is not good at filtering out or immobilizing wastes. Pollutants, if they happen to get into the water, can travel long distances. Industry or even extensive residential development in the central pinelands could spread contaminants widely through the underground reservoir.

Since the soils underlying the aquifer are sandy and porous, contamination is always a potential threat and would be pervasive throughout the enormous system.

Garfield DeMarco, cranberry grower and chairman of the Pinelands Environmental Council, concurs and suggests that the real battle in the Pine Barrens will come over water uses.

> I have a feeling that there will be a battle in the future. I don't see development—some housing here and there—agriculture and some sand and gravel operations. The real battle will come over its water uses. . . . I'm against transportation of water out of the Pines to the rest of the state. If there were people dying of lack of water, we'd have to look into it. . . . I don't think there's much of a threat of housing or development. Because of area remoteness—some hearty souls here and there—it's a little bit far for the average commuter. . . . The main state goal is to develop those water resources; otherwise I don't think the state cares about the Pines.

POPULATION & THE HUMAN ECOLOGY / 85

Local distrust of the state's plans for the water resource is reflected in an earlier document, the 1970 report of the study subcommittee of the Pinelands Advisory Committee of which DeMarco was also chairman. Here the committee reaffirms its territorial hegemony over the water sources:

> The New Jersey Division of Water Policy and Supply has consistently held that the vast underground reservoir of the Pinelands is to be used to meet the needs of South Jersey only and that this valuable resource should be preserved and dedicated to that purpose. The presence of this immense underground reservoir of pure water is of great importance to the southern part of New Jersey (Report 1970:3).

CONFLICT: MONOPOLIZING A VALUABLE RESOURCE

The conflict over land and water use is not so much over the goals of conservation versus development as it appears to arise from which level of organization manages the resources and therefore dictates resource policy. A pure and bountiful water supply is as essential to the cycle of cranberry growing and harvesting as it is to preservation as a source of water. Therefore, rather than conflict, consensus would be in order. The question is why does conflict exist over the need for water preservation? To analyze this question we first have to look at the local view as it stands in conflict with the state agency view.

Bill Haines is reported to be the largest landholding cranberry and blueberry grower within the state. His concern for state intervention stems from its interference of his autonomy in his agricultural practices:

> Most land is used for active agriculture. Use the other land for the watershed. We've got as much developed as we've got water to handle it. Polluted water's not good for cranberries. [possible pollution from off-shore oil drilling?] In Louisiana they use more water than we do and I don't think they have problems with oil. We're condemned a lot but I think we've done more to preserve the watershed. We get a lot of bad publicity cause we own a lot of land—they think we're land barons—land's here in my family for years and years. Take the Medford Lakes area. They took the cranberry bogs and made lakes out of them—built

86 / ENVIRONMENTAL DECISION MAKING

> homes around the lake and have a lot of them going down and saying you can't do anything with your land. A lot of people come here and get what they want and then they don't want anyone else to. It ticks me off; they say you can't do this or that and they done it. I say, if you want to protect the land buy it and pay taxes on it. They say they don't have the money [the environmentalists]. Put your money where your mouth is. They preserve the old town and I compliment them on it. . . . The 208 law on water pollution, I'm all for it. Keep the water potable; but the criteria don't make any sense—it's higher than the water is naturally. Evidently they're not very knowledgeable.

An agricultural agent familiar with the farmers and their problems points out that the fear of state water quality standards comes from the belief that the state would overregulate their business to the point of extinction, or accomplish the same purpose by land acquisition. Herbicides and fungicides are used to control the growth of "weeds that look like they came from outer space" and to control brown rot of the berries.

Haines comments:

> Somebody gets in an official capacity; they say you can't fertilize that bog cause there's phosphorous. These streams are not affected one iota by it. I'm a soil conservationist. That's the main part of it. . . . You can come in and look at it. That's what the state's been doing at Oswego Lake. The state's poor mouthing everything. We haven't got money to do this or that they say. They got the income tax. Thirty years ago the Pinelands ran from Marleton to the shore. Now they run from Tabernacle to Whiting with one heck of a lot of houses being developed in between. Agriculture centers have held land. I could sell every lot along Lake Oswego, on or up to Stormy Hill. I was offered a big price for 10-11 acres up there. But I don't think the state should come in here and say: "Look buddy, you can't do this or that" and steal the land we pay taxes on.

The acquisition of land by the state and the loss of ratables remains the rationale for distrust of the state's land and water policies. Garfield DeMarco, a large cranberry grower, refers to the water in terms of regional ownership:

Off-shore oil drilling? Because of experience in
other areas, we could probably handle it if there
isn't excessive damage. I'm against the transportation of water out of the Pines to the rest of the state.
. . . If you did extract water over a long period of
time it would change the ecology—it would end the
area as a cranberry and blueberry production area.
. . . If water is desperately needed in North Jersey—
if the economic survival of North Jersey depends upon
it—perhaps, but it would significantly change the Pines.
I'd hate to see a large section of South Jersey devastated
in order to provide water to the north.

The subcommittee of the Pinelands Advisory Committee, the parent of the Pinelands Environmental Council whose members included DeMarco, A. Morton Cooper, and W. Brooks Evert, noted in its 1970 report for the freeholders of Burlington and Ocean counties:

These significant accomplishments by the State [the development of recreational facilities at Lake Atsion,
Hampton Gate, Lebanon State Forest, Bass River State
Forest by the New Jersey Department of Conservation
and Development] were not carried out, however, without harming private landholders, counties and municipalities. Often land acquisition procedures were carried out in a highhanded fashion and little or no consideration was given. For example, Washington Township, Burlington County, was virtually obliterated; the
State acquired over 80 percent of this municipality and
because of the great loss of ratables the tax increased
by $8.76 to $17.36 in one year.

The concern for acquisition by the state and the example of the loss of ratables in Washington Township are discussed as reasons for fighting state water quality standards. State officials point out that the Washington Township loss was in actuality the state purchase of the Wharton Tract and that no such acquisition has occurred since that time.

The state officials acknowledge that water standards represent a means of monitoring open-space land; but both the State Department of Environmental Protection and the U.S. Bureau of Outdoor Recreation (BOR) of the Department of the Interior designate the land and water resources as having significance far beyond the purview of South Jersey.

Steve Picco, legislative director of the Department of Environmental Protection, notes:

> Water quality standards are the single most important regulation in the Pine Barrens. You can't change water quality in the Pine Barrens . . . it applies to surface and ground water supply. It had never before been applied to ground water in the state. The Pine Barrens are a critical area as far as sewers and septic tanks. Any construction for human habitation has to come to us under the critical areas bill.

Picco explains the position of the state agency and the federal agency on insuring the future water supply and recreation area:

> Insuring a future water supply source: It's the last major pure water supply in New Jersey or maybe in the Northeast corridor. Aesthetic arguments: the Pine Barrens' unique ecosystem. If you've got something unique, you want to preserve it. It's the last unique wilderness in the Northeast and it ought to be preserved. The same general preservation arguments apply at greater intensity. The center of megalopolis—maybe the Central Park of the future if that's the way development goes—one city stretching from Boston to Richmond and this one centers smack in the middle of it.
>
> The BOR is starting to realize on a federal level what we realize on a state level, that urban people need recreation too. Need it more. BOR money and Green Acres have been used in suburban areas where acquisition is easiest to develop. National-level BOR money has not reflected urban sensitivity—it has been out West in national parks rather than intensely developing urban areas like New Jersey. The Pine Barrens stands out like an oasis—maybe BOR realizes it's worth preserving.
>
> Given water quality standards, and wild and scenic rivers, legislation would result in a dormant arrangement. If we're going to protect the Pine Barrens it has to be an area absolutely inviolate. Something which has no deleterious effect on the water or aesthetics.

Conflict over the regulation of water stems from the realization on the part of local agricultural interests and state agencies that the regulation of water permits the regulation of land through which streams and rivers flow. As major landowners of the region, the large cranberry growers have been in a position to sell their land to developers, although a few like Haines and Thompson preferred to continue cranberry growing. The major difference between Haines' political alignments and those of his first cousin, Charles Thompson Jr., was that Haines saw state regulations as interference and harassment while Thompson saw regulation as the only possible means of preserving the land. Therefore, Haines participated in local political planning groups, such as the Pinelands Environmental Council, and Thompson and his attorney daughter Mary Ann supported the passage of federally sponsored legislation, such as the Florio bill to be discussed later. While Haines was appointed to represent agricultural interests on the Pinelands Environmental Council, Charles and Mary Ann Thompson drove from Vincentown at 5:00 in the morning to Washington, D.C. in order to testify in behalf of the Florio bill at the congressional hearings of the House Subcommittee on the Interior. Though both families continue in the old Quaker family tradition of cranberry growing as well as raising professional lawyers, they maintain opposing views on the control of cranberries and water. However, they understand that the growth of suburbs affects the already declining agricultural systems. This point is best illustrated in the examination of urban decentralization in the Pine Barrens region.

URBAN DECENTRALIZATION IN THE PINE BARRENS: HOUSING AND LAND

Urban decentralization was occurring at the same time as the decline of older systems of agriculture, and in New Jersey, as well as Long Island and Massachusetts, the decline of land utilized for the production of agriculture also produced residential and industrial development to widen the urban spheres in an ever-expanding ring.

To at least some of the inhabitants of the Pine Barrens region, abandoned farmland and woodland was a useless leftover in the landscape. In the crucial years following World War II, with the advance of urbanization, commercial entrepreneurs were searching for a means of profiting from the affluence and expansion of this urban field.

In Tables 5 and 6 we note evidence of the decline in percentage of open land within the two major counties, Burlington and Ocean, of the Pine Barrens region. The tables indicate over the two-decade

TABLE 5

Percent of Open Land (Farmland and Woodland) in Ocean County over Two Decades

Type of Land in Acres	Percent of County Area 1954	Percent of County Area 1971	Percent Difference
Total land in farmland	11.6	3.4	-8.2
Total land in woodland	4.9	1.1	-3.8
Combined total	16.5	4.5	-12.0

Note: Total county land is 410,240 acres.
Source: Compiled by the author.

TABLE 6

Percent of Open Land (Farmland and Woodland) in Burlington County over Two Decades

Type of Land in Acres	Percent of County Area 1954	Percent of County Area 1971	Percent Difference
Total land in farmland	40.0	32.0	-8.0
Total land in woodland	10.3	9.0	-0.9
Combined total	50.3	41.0	-8.9

Note: Total county land is 524,350 acres.
Sources: State of New Jersey, New Jersey Agricultural Statistics 1945-1956, New Jersey Crop Reporting Service, in cooperation with U.S. Department of Agriculture, July 1957; and Estimates of Land in Farms by Municipality and County, 1971.

period following the conclusion of World War II a loss of 10 percent of the combined counties' total farmland and woodland. Ocean County's loss of 12 percent of combined farmland and woodland between 1954 and 1971 is considerably higher than neighboring Burlington County, with a loss of 8.9 percent. The higher loss in open space is attributed to the Ocean County development policies for the growth of retirement villages.

SOCIAL CHANGE: RETIREMENT VILLAGES AS RURAL SUBURBIA

A large part of the growth in Ocean County during the past decade has occurred from the construction of retirement communities. Retirement villages meet the problems inherent in a rural region in transition. Senior citizens, largely retired, do not require access to urban centers, highly developed public transportation, nor the expansion of schools and facilities and therefore do not overload the limited services in the communities onto which they fringe. Of the county's growth from 1970 to 1976, 40 to 50 percent has been due to movement and resettlement of senior citizens in the areas.

Within that county, those townships squarely inside the Pine Barrens region—Manchester, Little Egg Harbor, and Stafford—contain a total of 7,993 dwelling units constructed since 1966 for retirement villages. The largest center for these villages, Manchester, contained a total of 7,910 dwelling units and seven retirement communities as of July 1976. The spread of development for retirement villages in Burlington County has already been in progress and serves to explain some of the current conflicts over land in Bass River Township. In addition, suburban housing for commuter families is also in evidence. Bass River Township in Burlington County attributes population growth from 737 in 1960 to 900 in 1973 to urban development. The township's population shows an increasing 20 percent proportion of senior citizens, as well as an increase in school-age groups. In addition, cranberry and blueberry growing provides too many problems for farmers, some of which are made dramatic by urban decentralization: the farmer has to resist attractive offers from developers to sell the land and get a good price for it.

Moreover, large landholders have cultivated all the land it is profitable to develop. They have reached a natural limit in their ability to farm land and make a profit. New technologies in cranberry growing and harvesting permit a higher yield per acre, and therefore less acreage is used to increase yield. In 1953, for example, Burlington County harvested 2,800 acres, 56 percent of the state's total devoted to cranberry growing, with a yield per barrel of 25; in 1955, 2,140 acres were harvested (59.4 percent of the state's total) with a yield per barrel of 28. Finally, in 1956, the county harvested a low of 1,800 acres (though a high state total of 60 percent) with an increasing yield per barrel of 27. As the yield increases, the land area available for harvesting decreases, given a relatively stable market. With such an increase in yield per acre, there is little incentive to harvest larger tracts of land.

The pressures to convert the land to other uses does, in turn, affect the preservation of open space in an urbanized region. An industrial society—more specifically, a highly developed industrial state—provides a structure of opportunities for the commercial use of land. There are no incentives in terms of tax structures or growth patterns toward the preservation of open space.

HOUSING AND NEW TOWNS IN THE PINES

The idea that open space was economically unproductive, a wasteland in an economically undeveloped region, was to rise again as a political and social issue with the proposal for New Towns in the Pines. New Towns as a community planning concept, noted in Chapter 3, began in England at the turn of the century but reached some development in the United States following World War I. The major component of a New Town was that it would be a planned community of limited density with economic self-containment. That self-containment was possible through the inclusion in planning of nearby industries and work settings, so that the separation of the place of work from the place of residence would be minimized, a phenomenon that Gottmann (1961) pointed out was the effect if not the cause of urbanization.

During the later 1960s the idea of developing New Towns as an alternative to the urban sprawl and mess was seriously considered by the federal administration. Once again, the local leadership in Pine Barrens communities saw the possibility of obtaining federal money for the planning and development of an industry— housing—requiring relatively inexpensive land and open space. Just as local leadership, freeholders of Burlington County, and mayors had applied for funds in 1959 to plan for an intercontinental jetport, in 1971 they were to apply for $50 million dollars of HUD (Housing and Urban Development) federal funding to plan for a New Towns community of some 80,000 occupants in Bass River Township.

BASS RIVER TOWNSHIP: A COMMUNITY WITHOUT CHANGE

The target site for the Pinelands New Towns was Bass River Township, an area of some 50,000 acres of open woodland from a total of 77 square miles in the southeasterly extremity of Burlington County.

The township forms a substantial part of the watershed for the Wading and Bass rivers, as well as the Mullica, into which they empty. All these rivers are in the center of the Pine Barrens. Bass River Township is an old Quaker settlement dating back to the early eighteenth century. As noted in Chapter 2, the iron bog industry was the basis of Martha's Furnace and Harrisville during the early 1800s, which was to decline some 50 years later when new technology—coal-burning furnaces—resulted in a shift of the center of smelting to the state of Pennsylvania. Other small-scale industries such as glass making and paper mills went through a cycle of development and decline until by 1900 all forms of industry and the settlements created to sustain them disappeared. The population that remained in this rural region moved into small-scale agricultural activities, mostly cranberry and blueberry growing; and into cord-wood and cedar pole production from the forests; shell and fin-fish production from Great Bay; and boatbuilding industries along the river.

The population density has remained stable and in fact reflects a decline from the preceding century. The density of the population is .02 person per acre and suggests the precarious balance between a limited economy and its population.

New Gretna is the village within the township that contains the majority of the population. It sports a main street with one restaurant, the New Gretna House, a dark-red wooden building whose deeper colored overhanging eaves slope heavily and unevenly with age. Just down the way on Main Street is a fire house. The local postmistress (who holds the job for life) conducts business from her home. Only the large American flag planted in the front grass indicates the existence of a government business. When the postmistress is finally relieved of her post, the post office will be set up in the home of the next lifetime appointee. No mail is delivered in New Gretna and a letter to the mayor, Floyd West, requires little more than the words "P.O., New Gretna, New Jersey," or simply, "New Gretna, New Jersey."

Across the road from the New Gretna House is an aging wooden building of similar vintage identified by the words "Pizza, Baked Goods." Clearly, that is not what the original builder had in mind, as an inner room was once the large meeting room of the former

Grange Hall. Neither the farmers nor the community meet in the Grange Hall anymore.

Community meetings are, at present, held at the local elementary school building and concentrate on the struggles over new housing, rising population density, and the demand for services to support the new settlers. The original battle, however, was generated by the plans for a New Town in the Pinelands in Bass River Township.

In 1971 Floyd West, a member of the Township Committee, quite by accident read an item in a Newark newspaper that plans for a new city in Bass River Township in the Pine Barrens had been approved by a federal agency, Housing and Urban Development. The news story indicated that there were no obstacles for a $50 million expenditure to start the engineering and design of a New Towns community for some 80,000 people. The population of Bass River as reported in the 1970 census was 815.

The plans to create New Towns in the Pinelands would explode Bass River Township's population to a dramatic 80,815. The enthusiastic report noted that a railroad spur would be started to connect Bass River with the tiny village of Chatsworth and that future plans would bring about an airport and a brewery to employ the arriving residents of this newly created, self-sustaining city.

West saw the New Towns application as a federal response to the political climate of the times. He felt it was a spurious solution to the student unrest and to the negative response to the Vietnam War. Thus, he pointed out that it was "a solution to the political problems after the riots . . . supposedly to solve all problems by providing a mix of all levels of economic strata. . . ."

If he was not sanguine about the idea of a New Town in Bass River, he was more immediately alarmed at the fact that even as a member of the Township Committee, this item in the Newark newspaper was the first knowledge he had of such plans in the works. He learned, after inquiry, that the then mayor was owner of some 7,000 acres of land in the heart of that proposed New Town. West gathered additional information with the help of a resident he describes as a "former CIA man" and confirmed the newspaper report. At this point, West began open political action against the mayor, the New Town, and the secrecy of the local government committee who were working to create a new city, replacing the village as it had been.

West is a soft-spoken man with a faint Southwestern drawl. He speaks fluently, even eloquently at times. He moved to Bass River when he married a woman from an old Pine Barrens Quaker family, and he exhibits a political sophistication worthy of urban settings. Once aroused by the report of the plans for the New Town,

West began to talk to the newspapers and to address public meetings on the secrecy in developing plans for New Towns, and though he roused a furor among the local citizens, he felt helpless about reversing the federal decision.

West consulted a lawyer and learned that New Jersey townships could have a choice of one of two forms of government, either a Township Committee or a Township Commission, and that a decision to shift structures could result in the total disbanding of the existing government. By obtaining signatures of 25 percent of registered voters, he could require that an election be held that could force a change in the form of local government and election of a new set of officials. West undertook this maneuver and was successful. Under the newly formed township commission, Floyd West was elected mayor of Bass River Township. His first act as mayor was to withdraw the New Towns proposal. In 1971 the doors were closed, at least for the time being, on large-scale housing development in Bass River Township.

PLURALISM IN THE 1970S

In the 1970s, housing was the major threat to existing open spaces. Just as in the 1960s airports and jetports were to generate opposition, conflict, and the political climate for interest-group development, the "threat" of housing development in the 1970s brought about newer forms of political engagement. In the Bass River Township incident, interest groups were no longer outside the governing structure but had become members of the legitimate governing or planning structures. The latter reflected and supported a consensus of the positions of the interest groups so represented.

The formation of the Pinelands Environmental Council by early 1970 (discussed in Chapter 5) reflected a similar move toward the inclusion of interest groups in official planning bodies. By the 1970s, political activism, regardless of whether the programs were "liberal" or "conservative," would find themselves operating within the formal governing or planning bodies.

The tools of the 1960s—the protest marches and demonstrations that characterized the antijetport activities of the Great Swamp interest groups and, to a lesser extent, the Pine Barrens people— were beginning to take new forms in the 1970s. There were fewer and fewer marches and demonstrations, but there was the birth of new planning bodies. This gave rise to the use of legal systems and legislation to establish cooperatives and formalize the power of interest groups. The result was that the interest groups were now operating as part of the existing governmental agencies. They were, in fact, learning to utilize bureaucratic agencies toward their own ends. Change was being generated from within the system instead of—as in the 1960s—being generated outside of it by public protest, demonstration, and implicit or explicit threats. Although new problems are present in the 1970s and 1980s relative to the persistence of open space in the Pine Barrens, the means of dealing with the problems rest upon the growth and cooperation of interest groups into quasi-governmental structures. This will be discussed in the following chapters.

PART II

THE ELABORATION OF INTERESTS– FROM PROTEST TO FORMAL ORGANIZATION

INTRODUCTION TO PART II

Significant technological changes in the post-World War II U.S. society intensified the scale and pervasiveness of industrialization and its by-products. These advances, in turn, created pressures for new uses of open land: The forces of economic development spurred the quest for new jetports in the early 1960s and for continually growing housing development in the total period after World War II. By the late 1960s and early 1970s a market for new housing was feasible in the Pine Barrens. The response of communities adjacent to the proposed advances, and of some old-line conservationists who organized at levels that cut across specific communities, was to organize loosely knit, issue-oriented protest groups.

In the 1960s, interest groups drafted letter-writing campaigns, organized demonstrations and protest marches, and raised money to hire attorneys to represent their viewpoints on the issues. In addition, these interest groups organized as political constituencies and created pressures on the legislative representatives to draft or oppose legislation. By 1970, political activism had come in from the cold. No longer generating pressure from outside the political system, interest groups began to enter the corridors of power.

Groups no longer simply dealt with one specific crisis: they had routinized their organizations, established stable memberships, hired executive directors, set up permanent offices, and participated in the creation of environmental policies. Significantly, they had shifted from a posture of protest to one of professionalism in planning.

Part II of this study deals with the second decade of conflict over land and water use in the Pine Barrens during the 1970s and into the 1980s. During the same period that interest groups moved from protest to participation in formal organizations, the fate of the Pine Barrens became subject once again to explicit public policy decision. Through the action and participation of protesters-turned-planners, and through the political sophistication gained in the battles of the 1960s, environmental interest groups and citizen planners worked with and against federal and state bureaucracies in arriving at institutional arrangements and new land management systems focused upon the Pine Barrens.

Thus, Part II focuses on interest groups and their emerging organizational strategies in this second era of environmental consciousness. It deals with the new forms of cleavage and cooperation that have emerged under the new systems of cooptation.

5

CLEAVAGE AND ORGANIZATIONAL STRATEGY

> The imperatives of technology and organization, not the images of ideology, are what determine the shape of economic society . . . although it will not necessarily be welcomed by those whose intellectual capital and moral fervor are invested in the present images of the market economy as the antithesis of social planning . . . nor their disciples who, with lesser intellectual investment, carry the banners of free markets and free enterprise. . . . Nor will it be welcomed by those who identify planning exclusively with socialism.
> Galbraith 1967:19

The main shift in the second era of Pine Barrens disputes was from the activities of protest groups and the repertoire of protest activities toward a structured, formal involvement with government planning bureaucracies, especially those of New Jersey. Before that point, the planning bureaucracies were exclusively government agencies.

The business communities that carried the banner of free enterprise had not only identified planning exclusively with socialism, they had entirely relegated to the government bureaucracies this seemingly negative function. The influence of post-World War II prosperity stressed the social efficiency of the unmanaged market and argued that business interference was considered damaging to the efficiency of the private sector. Thus Galbraith's wry comment on the "affluent society's" struggle for power with the state: "the most dangerously intrusive agency was the state. . . . The test of faith in the market, it followed, was the rigor with which one sought to minimize the role of the state" (Galbraith 1969:xii). These arguments were made despite the fact that continuously expanding federal and state budgets underwrote the "free" market as well as specific industries favored by these budgets.

Ironically, the first formally organized and legislatively established planning group, the Pinelands Environmental Council, was composed of the advocates of free enterprise, local control, and the gatekeepers of the private property interests in the Pine Barrens. Formed in 1970, the PEC's creation was closely followed by the creation of an opposing, and equally distinct, form of planning strategy on the part of the environmentalists, who embraced state and federal agencies in an attempt to win planning and policy influence in agencies outside the Pine Barrens and, in many instances, at the federal level.

Thus, in the 1970s, during the second era of environmental issues, there emerged a highly subtle form of power maneuvering whereby the official planning agency became the medium through which interest groups attempted to control land management policies. While the proponents of local control and free enterprise established, with state support, locally based planning agencies, the opposing environmentalists sought to involve the state and federal agencies as coplanners of the region. The subtlety of these planning strategies became more apparent as new planning groups and task forces were formed. The rationality for this kind of planning is often not easily explained, since it tends to be based on new forms of manipulation whereby formal planning agencies become simply the screen behind which interest groups attempt to dictate land management policies from interest and value bases that have little to do with planning as an exercise in rationality.

PLANNING AS A RATIONAL SYSTEM OF CONTROL

While sociologists have pointed out that both Weber and Manheim emphasized the rationality of bureaucracy and planning (Bensman and Lilienfeld 1973), it should be noted that Weber differentiated between the formal and the substantive. The differentiation was in terms of the clearly articulated formal procedure, and the substantive rationality in which concern is centered on substantive ends, with formal procedure being of instrumental importance.

With the increase of pluralism in and out of bureaucracies, interest groups participating in planning bodies, and the pressures that operate on the formulation of social policy, the question of whether an integrated, substantive rationality can govern modern planning has been posed:

Conceive of the state, the nation as a collectivity of
individuals and groups, classes, organizations, political
parties, each of which may have goals, interests,
ideologies, and structures of relevance which are
sometimes unrelated to each other and often in conflict,
then the goals within which planning takes place
are not to be regarded as given and are often defined
as articulated only within the process of planning itself
(Bensman and Lilienfeld 1973:299).

The ideologist of planning affirms that the planning process is
rational and therefore capable of producing a rational order; but beyond
the ideology of rational order, planning may in fact emerge
from the desire to extend the jurisdiction of an existing bureaucracy
or interest group. Therefore, one possible outcome of planning is
that the designated agent or agency extends its jurisdiction or advance
interests, either for itself or for some other agency or interest
group. The use of planning as a system of formal rationality,
then, can be to shift managerial jurisdictions from one level of government
to another as well as to extend the jurisdiction or influence
of an existing bureaucracy, and it can be used to advance the interests
of a nongovernmental interest group. This has been the case
with respect to the Pine Barrens.

In the Pine Barrens, the awareness of the need for planning
was absent until the late 1960s. Then local farmers, businessmen,
and conservationists recognized a potential shift in jurisdiction over
the area toward agencies of the state or federal governments and
away from their local bases of power. The existing local elites,
who had had primary influence in the area in the absence of these
higher jurisdictions, moved politically for the formation of an official
planning agency for the Pine Barrens that was locally and regionally
based and that would heavily represent their interests. If
planning was becoming recognized as a form for achieving rationality
in government, then the local interests too could plan and practice
the art of "formal" rationality. Thus the Pinelands Environmental
Council was born.

SYSTEMS OF LOCAL CONTROL IN FORMALIZED INTEREST GROUPS: THE PROPERTY OWNERS' STRATEGY

In the 1960s the locally based conservation groups organized,
as we have indicated, to preserve the Pinelands from the threat of
construction of an international jetport. Under the loosely knit

organization of locally based conservation groups, a coalition who called themselves FOCUS (Federation of Conservationsts United Societies, Inc.) worked quietly to see if a study could be made that would allow the Department of the Interior to designate the Pine Barrens as a region of national significance. Since the state government and the New York-New Jersey Port Authority were focusing on the establishment of a jetport, the old-line conservationsts argued, federal jurisdiction would limit and contain state jurisdiction; but they believed that the actual management of the land should be left to local interests.

Local agricultural businessmen in the Pine Barrens townships—some of whom served as local freeholders, and others who dominated the political networks that elected the freeholders—were not indifferent to these development proposals and policies. They were alarmed at the possibility of federal control. In 1969 the rhetoric of traditional agricultural and business fundamentalism began to be sounded throughout the Pines. Thus one planner participant recounted this story:

> . . . the word got out that the Department of the Interior was studying to see if they should make a park or national monument—that the national government was doing something in the Pine Barrens. Well, as soon as that got out everybody was really excited about it—"The feds are coming and we're going to lose our municipalities; we gotta keep the feds out of here"— and tempers flared so badly that people were flexing their fists at each other and making all sorts of remarks about the Department of the Interior, the Park Service, and anybody who had anything to do with it.

The local member of the PEC who related this story of panic and anger at the idea of federal control explained and justified his antifederal attitudes with the following remark: "New Jersey has a reputation of being a state with 'home rule' and people are very jealous of it—the ability to run their own business and not have some 'great white father' tell them what to do."

This expression of rugged individualism, of American populism, came, peculiarly, from the ranks of big business, the expanding agribusiness of the cranberry collective leaders. However, populism still has political importance to audiences in the Pine Barrens, despite the fact that the rhetoric no longer reflects the reality. For example, at a hearing in Chatsworth on proposed water quality standards, a man in his middle thirties who was later identified as a builder delivered an impassioned speech on local control: "We are the sons of those early pioneers. They were good and true people who farmed and loved the land. Now they want to take our birthright away from us."

That same evening, the chairman of the Woodland Township Planning Board, who had supported the development of a housing project in that township, offered a similar perspective:

> We are the native sons, rugged but good people. Our forefathers took care of it and preserved it now and they're being shoved aside by powerful warring factions. There has been little if any mention of those native sons of the Pine Barrens. These people are a cruel example of majority rule. People of the state are interfering and deciding the fate of the Pine Barrens. The state has ignored our needs and our plight. We cannot formulate policy without giving primary consideration to native sons.

The mayor of Washington Township, Earl Hill, stated his fear of state land ownership and control:

> I've lived here only 45 years. Who had this brilliant idea to draw a line around this whole thing [referring to proposed federal legislation for Green Line Boundaries]? The state owns 60 percent of Washington Township. Then they step in with the Wetlands Act to take another 20 percent. I'm going to take it to the Supreme Court—it's unconstitutional.

The irony of Hill's statement is reflected in his invoking of the Supreme Court and the Constitution as federal mechanisms for sustaining local control. The mayor of Shamong Township, Addison Bradley, repeated a statement often made by Garfield DeMarco when opposing the role of state control: "The parent, while appreciated, should let go of the reins."

One outspoken leader used stronger terms to define the role of federal and state agencies. He defined the control by governmental agencies as nothing less than "communism." Finally, a Burlington County freeholder, Robert Shinn, Jr., who was to later (1977) successfully float a bond for $1 million to purchase critically endangered lands in the Pine Barrens, noted that he was "against preservation in a practical economic standpoint." Shinn praised the policy of development rights that the Department of Agriculture was fostering, but noted categorically that he was against regulations.

Still another mayor, Henderson of Eagleswood Township, stood against state or federal regulations: "We want input into our own future destiny. We've lost acreage—your property rights. We in our town want control of our own destiny."

Opposed to this localism was Mayor Tully of Mullica Township, who described his area as "the most polluted township in the area":

> We do not have control of our own destiny locally and we need the state to help us. The lake [Mullica] smelled like unwashed diapers. In January we had the worst fish kill. Breweries run into the Mullica River. We're not on the public payroll . . . that stinking old sewage system should be knocked out.

In opposition to overwhelming interest in local control, the mayor of Bass River Township, Floyd West, equates local control with the increasing problem of urban sprawl:

> Urban sprawl could cause serious pollution to water, surface and underground. Can you change the course? The answer is yes . . . the government in New Jersey. The discharge of sewage into rivers is a concern to residents. The shellfish industry continues to suffer a loss. There are signs of irreversibility everywhere: Contaminated wells in Freehold, Mannville, Burlington County, Ocean County; lakes closed by pollution; real estate development is throwing sand in our eyes with a lot of irrelevancy.

Accordingly, West's suggestion that it was real estate developers who were throwing sand in their eyes implies that agricultural fundamentalism and antifederalism mask a more basic concern for rights of developers to make profits by despoiling the environment. The creation of the regional planning body, the Pinelands Environmental Council, would be a further indicator of property owners' and businessmen's strategy.

STRATEGIES OF THE PEC: POWER AND LOCAL CONTROL

The situation that evoked the fear of the "feds" in 1968 was the fact that Jack McCormick was writing part of his doctoral dissertation on the ecological significance of the Pine Barrens for the

National Park Service. The result of a fist-flying controversy in a meeting in New Gretna was a decision on the part of the county freeholders to form a committee, the Pinelands Advisory Committee. The goal of this group was to attempt to influence the Park Service study and the solutions suggested, proposed by the National Park Service, and perhaps even more importantly, to learn of the planning activities contemplated by the Park Service in the course of that study.

The committee examined the role of other regional land use commissions, particularly the Hudson River Valley Commission, and decided that that commission was not locally based or sufficiently represented by local interests. Commented J. Morton Cooper, an old-line conservationist who later was appointed to serve on the PEC: "The governor of New York could appoint any crony to oversee the Hudson River—maybe they never saw the Hudson—maybe they lived hundreds of miles away from it. . . ." Thus the committee reaffirmed the principle of home rule and recommended that members of the soon-to-be-formed planning body be appointed from the area.

There seems little doubt, given the principle of home rule in New Jersey communities, and the land management conflicts with state or federal control, that the county freeholders had different interests and priorities in planning from those of state and federal agencies. They were engaged in the process of pressure-group politics, the ends for which were agreed but outside the process of formal planning. What they felt they needed at this time were formal mechanisms that embodied home rule and the interests behind home rule.

With an ideology of home rule, a bill for the developing regional planning body, Assembly Bill 2096 (Chapter 417, laws of 1971), was drafted by Assemblyman Barry Parker to create the Pinelands Environmental Council.

Cooper and the Everts, all old-line conservationists who accepted appointment to the council, saw the legislation as a compromise. It carried no binding enforcement powers, merely the power to delay construction or development for a period of several months, pending review by the council. A deputy commissioner of environmental protection, Al Guido, disagreed with the idea that the drafting of the PEC bill was in any way a compromise by the property interests: "They got exactly what they wanted. There was no compromise. They could lead people in the state to believe that the Pine Barrens was being looked after while they went ahead and did exactly what they wanted."

The composition of the PEC through its appointments procedure reflected the dominance of a cast of characters already locally powerful and committed to home rule and local control over state and federal intervention. All appointments were made by the two freeholders of Ocean and Burlington counties. The chairman of the PEC represented the large cranberry and blueberry interests and was, of course, a large landholder. He was J. Garfield DeMarco, lawyer, cranberry grower, chairman of the Burlington County Republican Party, and representative of the Cranberry Growers Association. Bill Haines, the largest cranberry grower in the region, was named to represent the blueberry growers' interests. Morton Cooper, secretary of the council, was to represent the conservationists from Burlington County. Two representatives of the sportsmen's groups, one from each of the two counties, were appointed and the remaining five members were the mayors of each of the townships included in the boundaries defined by the council. These were the mayors of Eagleswood, Woodland, Manchester, Little Egg Harbor, Washington, and Bass River. Although some of these mayors may have been changed since the 1975 report of the council, the overall position on home rule and antifederal intervention persists, with the departure from that position by Floyd West, mayor of Bass River Township.

The lone figure on the council designated to represent the state government was the commissioner of environmental protection's representative, Howard Wolf, later replaced by Al Guido. The hired executive director was Joseph Portash, who was also the mayor of Manchester Township and therefore entitled to appoint his chosen representative on the council. The council produced a planning report, "Proposed Plan for the Pinelands, 1975," a plan that evaluated critical areas and developable areas.

A crisis emerged when the commissioner of environmental protection, David Bardin, identified this plan as a "developer's dream," since it proposed that zoning regulations in developable areas would allow half-acre lots. Cooper, speaking as a member of the PEC, noted that the zoning regulations to smaller units of half-acre lots was merely compliance with the recently passed Mount Laurel decision. This legal decision, known as the "antisnob law," outlawed the exclusion of small lots from zoning regulations as a means of including low income housing and people in heretofore closed middle class communities.

However, Commissioner Bardin concluded that the PEC planning document allowed the construction of more than 160,000 new housing units and that, moreover, it did not address itself to the problem of water pollution caused by resultant run-offs from streams, landfills, and sewage. In short, as a land and water preservation plan, it left much to be desired.

During the same period of time that the commissioner criticized the council for its special concern with private property rights, the executive director of the PEC, Portash, was to be indicted for conflict of interest when it was learned that he had served as paid consultant to a major retirement village builder while he had been both mayor of Manchester Township and paid executive director of the Planning Council. Even though Portash was indicted (on a lesser charge), the citizens of the township, particularly the senior citizens who inhabit the seven Crestwood Village communities in his township, gave support to their mayor as a "nice guy" who had simply moved into a newer home and had needed extra funds.

While the state agency spoke critically of the regional planning council, DeMarco, in his role as chairman of the PEC, wrote an angry letter to Commissioner Bardin (September 8, 1975). He spoke forcefully about the charge that the council served "private property" interests, and of the "elitist" attitudes of unelected state bureaucrats:

> I note your charge that the Council has overly concerned itself with traditional "private property rights." I am certain that many, if not most, Council members are concerned with "traditional property rights." Without these rights no one's home or farm holdings are safe from the elitist onslaught of administrative bureaucrats who cannot be reached by the electorate.

This theme of private property rights versus state and national social criteria regulating land use reappears in many of DeMarco's public statements.

Following the publication of the "Plan for the Pinelands," the state Department of Environmental Protection withdrew its half of funding of the PEC. Thereafter, relying solely on matching funds from the county freeholders, the PEC continued to operate until a court decision denied all legality of the council as long as their jurisdiction included state-owned lands. The Pinelands Environmental Council was to rise again, however. Following the gubernatorial election of 1977 and the enthusiastic passage of freeholder Shinn's bond issue for $1 million (to be used for land acquisition), the PEC was funded once again and reorganized with Cooper as chairman and DeMarco as another member representing cranberry interests.

Within a political framework, the PEC was born during Governor Cahill's Republican administration and was in this sense a Republican "gift" to a strongly Republican region. The response of candidate Cahill to local feelings on the jetport crisis in the 1970s was described at length in Chapter 3. Under a Democratic governor, however (Governor Byrne), the repayment of Republican votes was no longer necessary since it was assumed that it could not produce Democratic votes under any possible circumstances.

During a Governor's Conference on the Pine Barrens at Princeton on December 17, 1976, Governor Byrne announced that he would name a cabinet-level planning committee to replace the PEC. This committee would contain 15 members with statewide representation, and the idea received support from the lone Democrat on the Burlington County Board of Chosen Freeholders, Catherine Costa, Assemblyman Charles B. Yates of Burlington County, and State Senator Joseph A. Maressa. It was Ms. Costa who pointed to the basic conflict of interests when large landholders are charged with developing protections against overdevelopment. DeMarco, in turn, noted that the PEC had asked for the state acquisition of 25,000 acres of land as a measure of preservation. At this point in the meeting, DeMarco voiced his position to the governor: "If the governor would put the money where his mouth is we could have the preservation desired."

POLICY ADVISORY GROUPS

Bernard Greenblatt, in his book Responsibility for Child Care (1971), notes that the composition of policy advisory groups is a process that often involves the selection of members who may decide in good measure the policy conclusion already reached by an appointing agent "since the focus and emphasis of a task force's deliberations and recommendations reflect its composition. . . ." These comments relate to the formation of policy advisory groups on a national level, since this is where his study was focused, but regional groups, such as the PEC, are no less subject to those observations. Membership in the PEC was organized to reflect largely local interests and a high level of consensus was achieved through its brief life and subsequent rebirth. With the exception of Mayor West, the council was in agreement on the issue of local control. They represented, after all, the network of local interests and power. To have done otherwise would have undermined their own roles as decision makers and betrayed the interests they represented. The position of Mayor West as dissenter on the council is discussed in Chapter 4.

While the property owners were formulating strategies for local control through their creation of new, official planning bodies, the environmentalists were beginning to participate in state agency structures.

THE ENVIRONMENTALISTS: STATE
AND FEDERAL STRATEGY

Before 1975, environmental groups in the general Pine Barrens region were as locally based as the membership in the PEC. Environmental issues were debated within local "watershed" associations that were linked neither to national groups, such as the Appalachian Mountain Club or the Sierra Club, nor to state or federal agencies. Their activities usually focused on a single issue, such as pollution of an essential watershed by the advance of industry or housing to the region. Carol Barrett, an outspoken Camden resident who was largely responsible for the establishment of a Sierra Club chapter in the Pine Barrens known as the West Jersey Group, described in an interview her perception of the powerlessness of locally based, single-issue watershed associations:

> . . . the Newton Creek Conservancy Association, or the Big Timber Creek Watershed Association—they were little groups who worked on the same thing and they didn't win battles, then they lose interest and membership. You battle the sewer pollution and you don't get anywhere because of the politics controlling the regional utility commission; so that's how the Sierra Club got started.

The Newton Creek Conservancy, the group Carol Barrett had first joined to combat sewer pollution, was started in 1971 by the local DAR committee on conservation. The DAR, since the turn of the century, had been concerned with both the historic significance and the conservation of local areas, particularly those with roots in early America. Newton Creek, where Barrett lives, was settled in 1681 and contained the original burial ground of the Quakers who had set up plantations in the region. After the 1930s, when the county started to put in the first paved roads, Newton Creek was the site of suburban settlers from the Philadelphia-Camden area who viewed this remote area as a "cheap" Philadelphia suburb.

By 1971 the Newton Creek Conservancy was formed, in response to sewage pollution as a critical issue. Six plants were then discharging sewage into Newton Creek, which was the watershed for the population's water. Thus Barrett notes: "In 1971 we were all ready for an environmental movement in our community."

The formation of the locally based conservancy included local members of garden clubs concerned with industrial impacts on plants and flora, newly awakened women's clubs involved in civic activities, a young couple from Philadelphia training in architecture with Ian McHarg, and teachers and students from the local schools. There was at this point no link to larger governmental structures, even though the conservationists were continuously losing battles against utility commissions who were regionally based and politically influential.

When a member of the Newton Creek Conservancy, Dorothy Stokes, suggested that one member join the Sierra Club just to gain information, Carol Barrett felt it was an opportunity to amass political strength, "especially lobbying and political awareness," and invited Sierra Club conservation chairperson, Diane Graves, and the Central New Jersey chapter chairperson, John Greene, both of Princeton, to speak at a meeting.

Until the founding of the West Jersey chapter of the Sierra Club, the national Sierra organization had representation in the Pine Barrens only through the loose association of Princeton-based leaders whose residence was some 50 miles north of the Pinelands. Characteristically, the Princeton residents reflected the old wealth volunteerism of California-born Graves and the canoeing and conservation interests of university physicist Greene.

Barrett, whose husband worked in a supermarket in the Camden region, was acutely aware of the social class differences suggested by residence in Princeton and by Sierra Club membership: "Well, you know the reputation of the Sierra Club—overeducated, elite, academic, they have more money than anyone else—they can afford to be environmentalists 'cause they have the money." But Barrett, who earlier had been active with the Civil Rights Movement and the Peace Movement, understood the need for statewide connections. She saw that small groups were ineffective in lobbying for issues whose origins and solutions were on the state and federal level:

> . . . in the local groups, I could see that small groups were dying, withering on the vine. I saw that we had no power and they seemed to be compromised, that you need your horizons to be broader, and I realized these issues were worldwide. The "garden parties" were at a loss in dealing with pollution or with the state; the state has no problem brushing those people off—they just didn't answer their phone calls.

In thinking that the state agencies were unresponsive to nonpolitical local groups, Barrett understood the necessity for statewide connections to an activist organization familiar with the political structure of the state. She was also quick to grasp the idea that the "working class" members in environmental groups would participate only on a limited basis: "Working class will participate when it's in their own backyard, but they don't hang around." The original members of the West Jersey Sierra Club chapter in the Pinelands were the activists who had belonged to the original local associations. They joined the Sierra Club but, according to Barrett, they were not "Sierra Club-type" people. They tended to feel frustrated by Sierra Club policies; in fact, they didn't like being hemmed in by policy set at higher levels. The newer members of the club chapter were, according to Barrett, "the guy next door with a little bit of a conscience who had reached a point in his life where he could take an interest in his own community."

Camden County did not offer the environmentalist representation like Princeton professors, typical of most Sierra Club activists. Thus Barrett notes: ". . . outdoors type people—Pine Barrens activists—we didn't have them here. Camden County is not the mecca of conservation. The people here want three cars in every garage . . . people who work . . . corporate America. . . ."

When the Sierra Club chapter was formed in 1975 it listed a membership of 269 people. Though most members were from Burlington and Camden counties, others came from the southern third of the state, Gloucester, Salem, Cumberland, Atlantic, and Cape May counties. The problems that concerned the members of the newly formed West Jersey Sierra Club chapter were local ones caused by pollution, but these problems had statewide and national implications. Club members expressed concern with sludge-dumping into the ocean and sewage problems, both of which affected their local environment.

In the 1970s, locally based conservation groups in the Pinelands were increasingly alarmed at the environmental impact of industrial and residential growth of the region, but they were powerless in dealing with state agencies and utility commissions, since their power base was not connected to local political business networks or to state agencies. Their base of power was enlarged when they joined a statewide environmental group whose participation in state politics had been increasing during the decade. Diane Graves of Princeton's Sierra Club served, along with builders and local landholders, on a Water Quality Task Force organized by the State Department of Environmental Protection. Some environmentalists served as planners on task forces, and others lobbied for representation on major planning commissions, such as the Governor's Pinelands Review Committee, where they served together with builder-developers and local landholders. The representation of both the environmentalists and the property owners continued to be largely locally based, and they also practiced lobbying for participation on statewide planning bodies.

112 / ENVIRONMENTAL DECISION MAKING

The interest groups had shifted from the demonstration and protest politics of the 1960s to participation in formal organizations in the 1970s. The function of planning as a rational system of land and water management brought their participation into newly created governmental planning agencies and limited them as outside pressure groups.

UNEXPECTED ALLIES

Disagreement still occurs with individuals who are not connected to the local political network. The Thompsons, for example, are one of four independent cranberry growers who do not belong to the Ocean Spray Collective, of which 50 cranberry growers are members. They do not support local control of land use and water policy since they see this as a device for the encroachment on farmland. In 1976 the Thompsons learned, quite by accident, that approval had been given for the extensions of sewer lines adjacent to their cranberry bogs. A proposed housing development would, they feel, provide damage to the creek that supplies water for their cranberry vines. Increased population density would bring water pollution and vandalism by trespassers. They contended that farmers concerned with the continuation of cranberry growing should support state water quality standards, though they are uncomfortable with "bureaucratic" management.

Mayor West, whose leadership in defeat of the New Towns proposal noted earlier in Chapter 4, is a dissenter in his role on the Pinelands Environmental Council and as a mayor of a Burlington County township.

In both cases, the dissenting individuals are not connected to the political, agricultural, and business network that brings cohesion to the local associations identified. Perhaps their political ideas and interests disqualify them from acceptance by local elites.

CLEAVAGE OF ENVIRONMENTAL INTEREST GROUPS

One can attempt to determine the basis of environmental interest-group formation on the Pine Barrens; but a single dimension serves to explain the positions taken by individuals or the groups they represent. In the voluntary organizations a substantial difference exists between old-line conservationists and new environmentalists. Table 7 identifies the major differences between the two types of organizations.

TABLE 7

Interest-Group Formation in the Pine Barrens

Conservationists (old line)	Environmentalists (new line)
Organizations	
Audubon Society, national FOCUS, local	Sierra Club, national League Conservation Foundation
New Jersey Conservation Foundation	Littoral Society, state and national Appalachian Mountain Club
Coalition for Preservation of the Pine Barrens Founded, June 1977	
Chief Rationale for Preservation	
Conservation of resources	Preservation of wilderness and recreation value
Preservation of wildlife and wilderness setting	
Political Identification	
Republican	Democrat
Participation in Pine Barrens Policy	
Organization during 1960s jetport dispute	Not active in jetport dispute
	Major participation during 1970 conflicts

Source: Compiled by the author.

Although a South Jersey Sierra Club chapter was formed and activated in 1975, the original leadership of the environmentalists came from central and northern New Jersey. Membership in these organizations tend to be upper class with three or more generations of old wealth. Not all of the members of this status group are currently wealthy, however, even though they come from old families; these groups continue to oppose expanding industrialization. However, the central part of the state, where both Princeton and Rutgers universities exist, contributed members from the ranks of the faculty whose interest in environmental questions is both professional and personal. They are the canoeists and recreationists whose leisure activities are enhanced by the use of the Pine Barrens.

The newer South Jersey chapter has incorporated members with more modest incomes, middle to lower middle class, but the upper class image is still attached to them. In a June 13, 1977 letter in a local paper, the Camden *Courier Post*, the environmentalists were accused of fighting for "multimillion dollar scenic lands for the Affluent": "With the thousands of New Jersey citizens living in slums, freezing in the winter and burning up in the summer, barely getting enough food and clothing to exist on we must still have our multimillion dollar Pine Barrens and scenic lands for the affluent." The letters that followed in reply were from citizens who pointed out that they were not wealthy but concerned about the precious water resource. Wrote a man from Maple Shade: "I spent the crash of 1975 out of work. I am for more employment in New Jersey. I am for helping the poor and spending the tax dollars wisely. I am also for preserving the Pine Barrens at all costs" (Camden *Courier Post*, June 16, 1977).

Though resource preservation was recognized as a necessity of the less affluent, the notion of slowing industrialization and containing the self-interest of local landholders continues to be seen as self-interest of the affluent.

New environmentalists continue the nineteenth-century wilderness preservation policy. Industrialization and its impact on the remaining portions of open space is a movement they continue to oppose; in political partnership with federal and state agencies they lobby for public policy to contain economic growth. The old wealth is now joined by upper middle and middle income groups who themselves reside in suburbia, enjoy the recreation possibilities of open space reserves, and endorse the conservation of natural resources. The fight to save the Pinelands has become popular.

ANALYSIS OF POLITICAL ALIGNMENTS

Pine Barrens disputes were heightened by the gubernatorial election campaign of 1977, just as the region had become an open campaign issue in the mid- and late 1960s during the jetport controversy:

> For too long the Pinelands has been used as a political football, conveniently brought out of the closet and dusted off for the voters and just as conveniently put away after election. Public attention usually has penetrated to the depth of a nicely photographed picture from a helicopter fly-on—or a duly reported walkthrough—a "media event" (Speech by Congressman Edwin Forsythe, February 1977).

The jetport "threat" was nurtured by local, largely Republican leaders as the battle cry and rationale for the establishment of the unique, regional planning body, the Pinelands Environmental Council. The then Republican Governor Cahill supported his South Jersey Republican constituency and fostered legislation that established the PEC as a planning body.

Planning centers on the right to control and manage a given resource. In the Pine Barrens the resource is water, and through the control of water, control of land use. The planning conflicts focus upon which level of government gains control over the planning process. One group supports local control. In terms of interest groups they fall into the following categories:

Pinelands Environmental Council	local planning body
Cranberry Growers Association	local agricultural collective
Burlington County Freeholders	local government
Home Owners League of South Jersey	local industry
mayors of local townships	unit of local government

Each group does not necessarily represent unique and separate individuals. There are, in fact, large areas of overlap. For example, the leaders of the PEC are also leaders of the Cranberry Growers Association, and of local Republican associations, and of the Ocean Spray Collective. In short, power is centered within a very small group of individuals whose interests in local autonomy would also preserve their personal autonomy. As part of their activity in the region, they participate in local politics and help to identify and elect freeholders and mayors who most appropriately serve those interest groups. Therefore, at a public hearing, the local position on planning goals appears to reflect consensus and broad representation.

116 / ENVIRONMENTAL DECISION MAKING

Another group supports state or federal control:

State Department of Environmental Protection (DEP)
governor of New Jersey (Democrat)
Democratic assemblymen
independent environmental associations
Department of the Interior: Bureau of Outdoor Recreation;
  Bureau of Land Management

At the level of the state, machinery party politics tend to define planning goals. The DEP and its commissioner are appointed by the current Democratic governor. Policies of the DEP may emanate from the governor's office. Since legislators are elected and require a constituency, their support or nonsupport of state control of necessity reflects the views of the politically effective constituencies. It is evident that the constituency of the Democrats is not the local group identified as supporting environmental preservation in the Pine Barrens. This becomes clear when we note the legislation proposed by the Republican legislator, Congressman Forsythe. His bill proposes that local municipalities be compensated for tax losses resulting from land acquired for the purposes of preservation by the state and federal governments. This bill expresses concerns of local landholders that loss of land from the tax rolls leads to loss of ratables.

LOCAL CONTROL VERSUS FEDERAL CONTROL

Local control is a critical issue in the preservation and management of the Pine Barrens. Even old-time conservationists (as differentiated from more recently involved environmentalists, such as the Sierra Club) speak with ambivalence toward the need for government intervention to preserve the region while adding that they "don't want some Great White Father coming in here and telling us what to do."

The preservation of the region as a system of green acres amid urban and suburban development, as a recreational urban park, would seem to require the judgment of Solomon. The question is: What systems of land management would deal with the multiple issues of financing the purchase of land and of designating a system of management that does not alienate local and state authorities while the necessary federal agencies participate?

Chapter 6 addresses the question raised at this point. The chapter looks at the creation of state and federal policies that generate new planning commissions: the Governor's Pinelands Review

Committee, which existed from 1977 to 1979; and the current Pinelands Commission of the 1980s. The chapter chronicles the ensuing battles of interest groups and newer actors in the struggle over environmental decision making to the present, 1981. Finally, it appraises the various state and federal partnership plans that emerge as innovations in the drafting of land management policies.

6

EMERGING INSTITUTIONAL ARRANGEMENTS FOR LAND USE POLICIES

> I was born here and . . . I guess its close to God and nature. . . . We figured it would always be ours but now we find out it's not. We didn't have the money to purchase it . . . and we figured nobody would and all of a sudden—bang—everybody's bought and a lot of them are developers.
> Statement of Gladys Eayre, Piney

In his study of conflicts between conservation and economic growth or development in the land and water policies of the state of Florida, Carter (1974) addresses himself to the problems of maintaining essential or desirable natural ecosystems in the endlessly complex subject of growth policy and urban development.

His findings resemble the New Jersey issues: the search for available open space in the 1960s for the development of an international jetport, the development of a nuclear power plant, construction of new housing after World War II and rising valuation of real estate, and endangered ecosystems through the introduction of industrial pollutants. Thus Carter (1974:6) concludes: "In many places, Florida was becoming dominated by the artifacts of an urban civilization in which nature was too often only grudgingly admitted."

Eight hundred miles northward in New Jersey, the Pine Barrens had moved from political conflicts centering on the search for an international jetport in the 1960s to the battles over land and water management in the early and mid-1970s. The cause of these pressures over the two-decade period was to some extent attributable to the changeover in the use of land and water from a rural, agricultural society to one that became an extension of the urban field. There was a decline in the use of land as farmland and a rise in the development of housing.

In the state of New Jersey between 1954 and 1964, 400,000 acres, or 24 percent of the 1954 total agriculture acreage, went out of production, and between 1964 and 1974 an additional 265,000 acres were retired from agriculture (Untaxing Open Space 1976:142).

The decline in farmland in New Jersey has been attributed to the high cost of maintaining farmland within the state's property tax structure. At least until 1976, when Governor Byrne passed the first New Jersey income tax, the state relied heavily upon the property tax. In fact, taxes per acre on farm real estate have been higher in New Jersey over the past 20 years than they have been in any other state. The tax structure itself appeared to favor urban development over agriculture since land even in agriculture is assessed at the full market value.

FARMLAND ASSESSMENT ACT

In 1964 the State Department of Agriculture enacted the New Jersey Farmland Assessment Act, which would attempt to apply use-value assessment to agricultural land. Use-value assessment would not forgive taxes, rather it kept assessment in line with net income from the land, permitting the farmer the opportunity to pay local taxes from present production (Luke 1976).

After the passage of the Farmland Assessment Act, between 1964 and 1974 the increase in farm real estate taxes continued but was slowed down considerably. Thus Luke's analysis of the first decade of the act noted a dramatic slowdown in the increase in qualified farmland taxes, "ranging from an increase of 2 percent in transitional areas to 33 percent in rural areas" (Luke 1976:4).

Problems arose as to whether vacant lands and forests were to be considered part of "active" agriculture. This was particularly important in the Pine Barrens, where most of the land is not directly devoted to the growing of cranberries and blueberries, but to the preservation of the water supply that made such growing possible. The result was that the definitions had to be rewritten: ". . . the qualification of vacant land with trees, oversized residential wooded tracts, and other forest tracts growing in woods challenge the concept of 'activity devoted to agriculture'" (Luke 1976:5).

Critics of the Farmland Assessment Act, Kolesar and Scholl (1975a; 1975b) maintain that it is precisely this ambiguity in definition that provided a preferential tax assessment for developers as well as farmers. They argue that development depends first on the existence of a market for housing, not on the property tax:

> It is a wonder now that anyone ever thought preferential assessment could preserve agricultural open space. The law was sold to the public on a mistaken premise . . . that high property taxes were causing development of farmland. It is obvious that development depends first on existence of a market for housing, factories, and stores. If the market is there, and if the zoning, sewers and mortgage money are available, development will take place regardless of any property tax breaks. If one farmer will not sell, another will. A tax saving of $40 an acre is of no moment when profits of thousands of dollars an acre are at hand (Kolesar and Scholl 1975a:25).

While collusion was not the intended function of the Farmland Assessment Act, since it was conceived as a realistic means of slowing down the process of agricultural decline, it may have provided, as an unintended consequence, new opportunities for housing developers. In the Pine Barrens, the fact that developers may have profited from the farmland tax assessment and its accompanying ambiguities would result largely from changes in land ownership that preceded these attempts at agricultural preservation. Developers and development interests had been quietly purchasing large tracts of forests and woodland prior to the passage of legislation and other institutional arrangements designed to preserve the open space.

High property taxes may have contributed to pressures to develop, although it was not the most important cause. The large cranberry farmers acknowledged that the Farmland Assessment Act had helped them considerably. The question was whether arduous farming and agricultural practices could compete economically with the sale of land to developers. For example, one cranberry farmer was forced to retire, partly because years of continuous work in icy cranberry bogs had accelerated a crippling arthritis in his hands. By selling his land to developers or developing it himself, this farmer might retire to live in Florida, though in this case it did not happen.

Those farmers who resist selling their property see the land either as falling into the hands of developers or coming under close management by the state. Mary Ann Thompson, daughter of cranberry grower Charles Thompson, favored management by a state agency. "It's either the developers or the state. I'd take the state 'cause at least you can lobby with them—with developers you can't do anything." When Mary Ann Thompson refers to the state, she is generally referring to the state agency, the Department of Environmental Protection, whose land use regulations center on control of the water, particularly ground water, in order to limit industrial development.

THE CONTROL OF WATER: STATE ARRANGEMENTS FOR LAND USE

The land use practice in the Pine Barrens is the product of institutional arrangements that control the stabile systems governing a watershed. The core of that system is the Mullica River into which all other rivers eventually flow: the Batsto, the Wading, and the Bass River flow into the Wading River. Charles Thompson, Jr., a cranberry grower and a member of one of the oldest families in the business, notes in an interview with this author the importance of that river: "Everybody's fortunes are tied up with the Mullica—that is, everybody north of Woodland Township and east of Warren Grove Road."

The ground water designated area of the Proposed Non-Degradation Water Quality Standards for the Pine Barrens Area (1976) will underlie the following surface water drainages (see Map 2):

a. Mullica River and all tributaries upstream from head of tide.
b. Cedar Creek and tributaries upstream from head of tide.
c. All fresh waters west of the Garden State Parkway bounded by the Mullica and Cedar Creek watersheds.
d. Toms River Watershed
   (1) Davenport Branch and tributaries upstream from Route 530.
   (2) Michaels Branch and tributaries upstream from the east crossing of the Penn Central Railroad.
e. Rancocas Creek Watershed
   (1) Burrs Mill Brook and tributaries upstream from Burrs Mill Pond at the Southampton-Woodland municipal boundary.

As a second attempt at institutional control, the state commissioner of environmental protection added the Mullica River-Chestnut Neck Historic District of Atlantic, Burlington, and Ocean counties on the State Register of Historic Places.

MAP 2

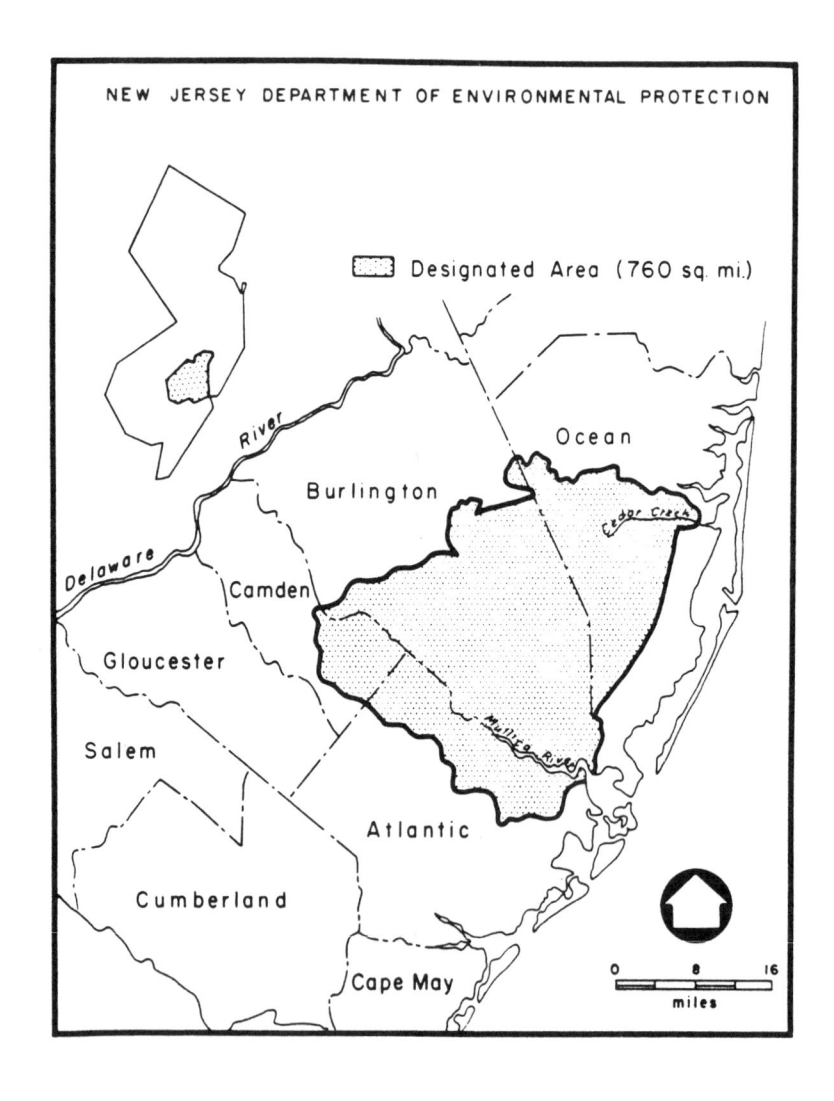

Pine Barrens Area Covered by Proposed
Water Quality Standards

Source: New Jersey State Department of Environmental Protection.

FROM PROTEST TO FORMAL ORGANIZATION / 123

The State Register is a list of properties and areas worthy of preservation for their historic, cultural, architectural, or archaeological distinctions. Inclusion on the register makes an area eligible for federal historic preservation funds. Register sites also have some measure of protection from government-sponsored encroachments (News release, DEP October 4, 1976).

A third attempt at institutional control, this one by the legislature—Assembly Bill A1992, the New Jersey Wild and Scenic River Act introduced in May 1976 by Assemblymen Stewart, Herman, Perskie, and Bassano—authorizes the establishment of the New Jersey Wild and Scenic Rivers System: "providing for the acquisition, designation, administration, and regulation of such rivers and their designated adjacent areas; and relating to the powers, duties, and responsibilities of the Department of Environmental Protection."

In effect, the bill provides for the use of power of eminent domain by the state agency over land within and around the rivers so designated.

> The department may use for the purposes of the system lands owned by the State, with the concurrence of the head of the administering agency, and acquire scenic easements in such lands by written cooperative agreement, donation, or purchase with donated or appropriated funds, or agree to manage any such lands in a manner consistent with the provisions of this act. . . . The department may acquire scenic easements in the name of the State within the designated boundaries of any river area of the system by the exercise of the power of eminent domain in the manner provided in P.L. 1971:c.361 (C.20:3-1 et seq.), without the consent of the owner, where, in the judgment of the commissioner, all reasonable efforts to acquire such scenic easements by negotiation have failed (Assembly Bill No. 1992, p. 4).

The act is a powerful piece of legislation that would give the state management powers over land via water quality regulation.

A fourth system of institutional control, at the federal level through the Department of the Interior, Bureau of Outdoor Recreation (BOR), has been assessing the "national significance" of the land and water system at the request of the State Department of Environmental Protection.

As a fifth system of institutional control, the professional environmentalists, the quasi-public/private sector under the leadership of the New Jersey Conservation Foundation, while awaiting the passage of legislation and regulations, have been raising funds and buying up tracts that state, federal, and private agencies have identified as having especially distinctive geologic, aquatic, or vegetative values. The foundation then sells them to a state agency as a means of assuring their permanent preservation.

The executive director of the New Jersey Conservation Foundation points out that this is part of a teamwork strategy:

> The United States Bureau of Outdoor Recreation, which has studied the Pine Barrens at length and endorses preservation, urges quick purchase of key areas while New Jersey legislates needed regulation of water, land and air resources, along with recognition that the Barrens is a nationally significant ecological region. Such steps should open the door to some Federal financing (New York Times, December 5, 1976).

Federal financing of land acquisition is the sixth system of institutional control. As a key speaker at the Governors' Conference on the Pine Barrens (Princeton, December 17, 1976) John Crutcher, director of the BOR, noted that the Land and Conservation Fund would be doubled the next year and tripled in 1980 so that they would be able to render more assistance to the Pine Barrens and other conservation areas.

On a seventh measure of institutional controls, Governor Byrne announced at that same conference that he would name a cabinet-level committee to make sure "no state action harmed the Pine Barrens environment."

As a final measure of institutional control, the governor proposed legislation that would restructure the Pinelands Environmental Council to more fully represent statewide interests, and thus apparently dilute the power of local interest groups.

The nine measures of institutional control and arrangement are both intense and relatively recent innovations. Most of the above-named measures, regulations, restrictions, and legislation were drafted between 1975 and 1977, with the major input coming during the year 1976. One would have to ask this question: Why such intense moves toward regulation over a two-year period, after years of legislative inactivity?

First it must be noted that seven of the nine measures are designed toward greater control and regulation of land via water by the state agency, the Department of Environmental Protection. Second is the intervention of federal agencies and legislation. Local control is a critical issue in the preservation and management of the Pine Barrens. Even old-line conservationists speak with ambivalence toward the need for federal intervention to preserve the region. The preservation of the region as a system of green acres amid urban and suburban development, or as a recreational urban park, is full of complexities and contradictions.

FEDERAL PARTICIPATION

A number of legislative plans have been formulated during the past two years whose goals were to manage, contain, control, or develop the Pine Barrens. A highly innovative concept was introduced by Congressman James Florio, a southern New Jersey legislator whose membership on the House Interior Committee's Subcommittee on National Parks and Insular Affairs made the passage of legislation a distinct possibility.

Congressman Florio has suggested the organization of Green Line Boundaries, a concept for preserving recreational landscapes in urban areas, in this case the Pine Barrens, so that existing activities of farming, or housing, will not be swallowed up by the regulations of a national park system. New development is prescribed, however. Concurrently, the recreational and resource areas remain protected and the character of the landscape is retained.

Such an approach, the creation of a Pine Barrens National Ecological Reserve, joins federal, state, and local governments cooperatively to apply a range of land acquisition and regulatory techniques. The Florio bill attempts to develop consensus between different agencies that control land use as a means of maintaining the dwindling natural lands and resources within an urbanized region. For the Northeastern seaboard where land is a valuable commodity in the marketplace, a concept for preserving the rural environment gives importance to that environment unheard of since the beginnings of industrialization.

In his statement before the House on April 20, 1977, Florio cited the Report of the Outdoor Recreation Resources Review Commission: "The commission's report, issued in 1962, helped to bring about the recognition that natural beauty, ecological balance, and the healthful use of leisure times are essential in an urban nation."

The preservation of a natural landscape meets more than a single societal requirement: one certainly is the preservation of the natural resources; but a second issue is the continuance of open space for the recreational needs of people themselves: urbanites, suburbanites, and rural dwellers. This point Florio makes clear when he designates landscape resources as a right of all Americans: ". . . the Commission's report affirmed the right of all Americans—including urban Americans—to the protection of landscape resources which possessed important ecological, scenic, and recreational values."

WHAT THE FLORIO BILL AUTHORIZED

The Florio bill (H.R6625) set the following guidelines for funding and management:

> Authorizes the secretary of the interior to provide grants to the state to cover 75 percent of the cost of developing a comprehensive land use plan, including the establishment of a commission, which would manage the plan.
> Directs the secretary of interior to establish guidelines for the land use plan, requiring it to include provisions for scenic, conservation, and recreational uses.
> Gives the secretary the right to acquire up to 50,000 acres of ecologically critical land and transfer it to the management commission's jurisdiction.
> Establishes a 13-member citizens' advisory commission, appointed by the governor, to assist the management commission in its work.
> Authorizes $50.5 million for land acquisition, management grants, and plan development.
> Provides the secretary of the interior ultimate oversight responsibility to insure the state management commission adheres to the approved state plan.
> Authorizes payments in lieu of taxes to local governments where acquisition of property results in actual loss of revenue.

The legislation may well have been a landmark in public policy. For New Jersey, a Northeastern urbanized state, a leader in the race toward unlimited growth and industrialization, the Florio bill made planning and controlled growth a high priority of public policy.

The congressman was not alone in his thinking. The concept of green line boundaries was generated by Charles E. Little of the Congressional Research Services and is at present in application along the northern edge of the megalopolis in the Adirondack Park System.

Reestablishing boundaries, such as the Green Line parks, in order to control development in the Pine Barrens seemed to have been the next step in the struggle to contain open space. Support for the legislation existed among the newly formed coalitions of conservation- and preservation-minded interest groups. One immediate issue was the composition and role of the citizens' advisory commission as a planning and enforcing body. Once again interest groups would participate as planners who would function within the governmental system to define the boundaries of the Pine Barrens and, in the process, will define the legislation itself.

THE GOVERNOR'S PINELANDS REVIEW COMMITTEE: 1977

In 1977, with the waning influence of the Pinelands Environmental Council, Governor Byrne appointed a 15-member committee whose goal it was to delineate boundaries for the Pine Barrens and to recommend preservation and protection policies.

The casting of this committee was somewhat broader than the earlier, locally based PEC. There were also representatives of northern and central New Jersey counties, both of the development and environmental protection factions. Craig Yates, brother of Burlington County assemblyman Charles Yates, was named chairman; Gary Patterson of the Pine Barrens Coalition was vice chairman; and Richard Binetsky of the State Department of Community Affairs was executive secretary. Dominick Cassetta, Jr., and Thomas Darlington represented the agricultural interests, while from the state government, Tom Hall represented Secretary of Agriculture Alampi. Charlie Goodman was a former mayor of the barrier reef region; Tom Hickey, a former engineer and newly minted lawyer from North Jersey was working in environmental law, as was Tom Norman as a South Jersey lawyer who focused on township disputes; Pete Lafen was a lawyer who first represented broad-based environmental associations, and was to later join Congressman Florio's staff in Washington; Nan Walnut and John Hiros represented local watershed associations as environmentalists; and Bill Ridgway and Dick Sambol, the New Jersey Home Builders Association of South Jersey. Karl Kehde was an upstate expert on building, and the two who resigned in 1977 were the architect, Malcolm Wells, and the Princeton lawyer, Bill O'Shaughnessy. Finally, Joan Goldstein, this author, was appointed a member of this committee as an expert on Pine Barrens issues.

128 / ENVIRONMENTAL DECISION MAKING

On the governmental level, two key state agencies were appointed and were dominant in the steering of the committee, providing a subtle tension between agencies and citizen appointees and toward its conclusion, between the two agencies themselves. The first agency was the Department of Community Affairs, represented by Ed Cornell, assistant commissioner of community affairs, and Dick Ginman, state planning director. The second state agency was the Department of Environmental Protection, and its representatives were Betty Wilson, a deputy commissioner, and Sean Reilly, their Pinelands coordinator. A third agency, the Department of Agriculture, was left to the rational input of its appointee, Tom Hall, a political scientist and a planner who eventually left the committee to work in the governor's planning office.

The two state agencies, Community Affairs and Environmental Protection, vied with each other for the ultimate planning responsibility of the Pine Barrens, and particularly so when the federal legislation fostered by Senator Williams placed a significant amount of planning responsibility and funding into the discretion of the state government and, more particularly, to the governor. This point underscores the issue of land planning moving to higher and higher levels of government, even while there is citizen participation. For example, in the next commission, which was to be formed from the Williams legislation, the new group would include an appointee of the secretary of the interior, as well as seven by the governor, and seven by local freeholders of those counties so designated as within the Pine Barrens boundaries.

This last issue of establishing boundaries was a charge of each of the planning groups established; with each succeeding committee, not only do the planning groups become more broadly based, so do the boundaries so delineated, as they encompass more and more of the Pine Barrens territory. This widening of boundaries serves to dilute the purview of current local interest groups.

THE HARRISON WILLIAMS SOLUTION: THE
PINELANDS PLANNING COMMISSION, 1979

With the passage of the Senate Omnibus Parks Bill in the final session of 1978, Senators Harrison Williams and Clifford Case made possible Pine Barrens planning legislation that stretched beyond local and state representation to include the Department of the Interior in Washington, D.C., though only one member of this new commission would represent the secretary of the interior. In addition to broadening the levels of government involved in the planning mechanism, the bill widened the relevant portions of South Jersey to include Atlantic, Camden, Cape May, Gloucester, and Cumberland counties. This is a striking contrast to the first committee's circle of Burlington and Ocean counties, areas that critics of the PEC have charged were the political stomping ground of those local leaders who tended to dominate the council. The outcome of this enlargement in boundary and representation can be studied only in the future, as decisions and mechanisms for preservation evolve from the intermixing of commission members and government agency representation. No doubt, they too have their agendas.

THE PINE BARRENS IN THE 1980s: INTERVENTION AND CRISIS

The year 1978 was an important one for the Pinelands. The Governor's Pinelands Review Committee (PRC) presented its planning and management report to the Byrne administration and was to be phased out of action.

It was the recommendation of the PRC that the region be organized along the concept of protection areas and preservation areas. They were visualized as a circle within a circle in which the center ring would be designated as a preservation area, that is, an area with government restrictions on construction or development of any kind; and the outer ring, the protection area in which controlled development could occur under the aegis of a planning commission. Moreover, the designated Pine Barrens boundary area had been enlarged considerably from the PEC maps of the early 1970s. Only ten years earlier, the PEC had restricted the boundary delineation largely to Burlington County with adjoining segments of Ocean County. The total Pinelands Planning and Management district now encompassed 1.10 million acres, of which 365,000 acres were in the preservation area. In addition, parts of Camden, Cape May, Cumberland, and Gloucester counties were added to the circle. (The most recent commission, the Pinelands Commission, has delineated the preservation area an increased 380,000 acres, and the protection area 730,000 acres, leaving the overall figure at 1.11 million acres.)

The problem that concerned many of the outgoing PRC members during the final days of the committee's existence was: How to control the expansion of land use activities until such time as the recommended regulatory mechanism and commission would be legitimated? Surely, if land speculation and manipulation were to occur, there was no better time than during the hiatus between planning and implementation. The "grandfathering" of prior acquisitions for development did in fact occupy the state Department of Environmental Protection for some time afterward.

The question of declaring a moratorium upon all further activity was presented as the solution by PRC member Charlie Goodman. Nevertheless, though the PRC had argued the question of a moratorium on construction until the promulgation of a master plan, the committee (this author included) was surprised to learn that the Byrne administration was to take strong affirmative action on the issue. On February 8, 1979, by means of an executive order, Governor Byrne imposed a moratorium on construction within the Pinelands designated boundaries until such time as the Master Plan would be drafted and in effect.

Challenged by development interests for legitimacy through the use of an executive order, the moratorium on construction was to find legislative muscle through the action of Senate President Joseph Merlino. These actions, in turn, produced endless hearings at the State House with testimony presented from all the divided interest groups. At this point, the state government, particularly the governor, rather than the federal government, became the target of opposition from development interests. Moreover, agriculture interests reacted to the overriding of their political hegemony in the region. The Agriculture Committee of the New Jersey legislature argued vigorously against the governor's actions and considered engaging in some political opposition until one member, Assemblywoman Barbara McConnell, lobbied for support of the governor.

By June 1978, in concert with Secretary of the Interior Cecil Andrus, and with political support from Congressman Florio and the Case/Williams bill, Governor Byrne signed the Pinelands Protection Act in which Congress designated the area as the Pinelands National Reserve. At a bill-signing ceremony held at the State House in Trenton, Byrne was ceremoniously presented with a sack full of pine cones, which he playfully tossed to members of the assembled audience.

That act carried the plan of the PRC one step further in terms of land management systems. Significantly, the plan provided funds for the state to produce a management plan, and for the establishment of a Pinelands Commission to devise the plan and ultimately to administer the region. As an added note of caution in the state/federal partnership, the act provided for the possible stewardship of the region by the Department of the Interior should the state fail to provide an adequate plan for preservation within the time limits stated.

The assembling of the new commission occurred within an intense political climate since the power of this commission carried the weight of millions of dollars in federal funding, and the enlarged powers of a commission. People were selected on the basis of regional and interest group representation; but only a small handful of the knowledgeable PRC committee members were to remain. New members of the Pinelands Commission were appointed because, according to one governor's aide, "they had a history of working with political issues." Thus, as the commissions were assembled with increasing decision-making power, those members chosen were themselves even more politically based than had been the case with prior citizen committees.

The Master Plan of the new Pinelands Commission presented to Governor Byrne on November 26, 1980, called for the protection and preservation ring concept posed by the former PRC committee, but the boundaries were once again delineated. This Master Plan divided the Pine Barrens into an inner 368,000-acre Preservation Plan, in which development is virtually banned, and a 780,000-acre outer Protection Area, in which building, development, and exploitation are controlled by designated regulations. This plan generated new conflicts with development and some agriculture interests. At this point, stories about the Pinelands crisis appeared on the front page of the New York *Times.* One such story, entitled "Pine Barrens Plan Stirs Furor on Land Use," makes the following observations about the now-included Mays Landing segment: "This rural Hamilton Township community of about 2,500 people exemplifies the controversy because of its proximity to Atlantic City and the spreading demand for housing created by the new casino industry there" (New York *Times*, January 13, 1981).

The story goes on to note that developers have bought up large tracts of land with plans for 30,000 housing units that would add 90,000 residents to the 9,800 currently scattered over some 115 square miles. Continues the *Times* article: "Such growth would be sharply limited by the state's conservation plan if it is approved by the Federal Department of Interior and enforced by the New Jersey Pinelands Commission."

Accordingly, the plan was presented to outgoing Interior Secretary Andrus for approval, which in turn would release an initial $26 million for purposes of land acquisition and administration. Governor Byrne at this point was racing against a new deadline: with the defeat of President Carter at the polls in the 1980 election, earlier agreements might not be adhered to under the upcoming administration. It was just under the wire, in the final day of the Carter White House, that Secretary Andrus approved the plan. Thus, the mechanism for a state/federal partnership in the management of an ecologically sensitive rural region had been enacted.

Significantly, the new management plan took root in the new decade of the 1980s; and it represented an important turn of events in the process of planning and environmental decision making for those peculiar pockets of rural locales set within the urban regions.

Commenting on this turn in the road in the struggle for the drafting of institutional arrangements for land management, State House reporter Dan Weissman, a Newark Star Ledger journalist, made the following observation to this author in an interview:

> The basic change is that the State has statutory power to regulate the area. They never had that before. The Pinelands Environmental Council was almost an excuse. They didn't have direct authority—only to advise and delay—but they couldn't take affirmative action. This group [the Pinlands Commission] is a review agency. You don't do anything without their approval. . . .

This new role of the state government to create and enforce land use control mechanisms, albeit in partnership with the federal agencies, comes as one kind of land management solution of the 1980s. Thus Weissman comments: "In years to come, there will be continually raging arguments over whether Byrne rewrote land use law."

Acquisition, in fact, has become the major function of the State Department of Environmental Protection with respect to the Pine Barrens designated Preservation Areas. Armed initially with Green Acre funds, shortly after the February 1979 moratorium on Pinelands development activities, the state DEP under Commissioner O'Hern and Deputy Commissioner Wilson created a unit within its Green Acres agency to deal specifically with Pinelands land acquisition. Howard Wolf was charged with acting on the acquisition of those areas identified as being environmentally and ecologically critical. According to current Commissioner Jerry English, the "DEP has developed an overall calendar that calls for acquisition of 96,000 acres in the next five years. So far, both the funding commitments and the anticipated acquisitions are on schedule."

What emerges as one examines the course of land acquisition in the Pine Barrens is a twofold pattern: the acquisition of land adjacent to rivers and potable water systems, thereby protecting and controlling water resources; and the acquisition of land contiguous to state-owned forests and parks, thereby enlarging those recreation areas and the state holdings. A good example of this point is to be found in the acquisition of Cedar Creek, some 261 acres purchased at a cost of $3,218 per acre, or a total of $840,000. DEP spokesmen point out that the new area links Double Trouble

State Park to the Greenwood Forest Wildlife Management Area and Lebanon State Forest. This pattern of contiguous acquisition actually doubles the state's purview of land and water management systems. The following table demonstrates the point:

Cedar Creek

Existing areas	Acres
Double Trouble State Park	1,614
Pasadena Wildlife Management Area	3,119
Greenwood Forest Wildlife Management Area	8,958
Estimated acquisition area, Phase I	1,500
Estimated acquisition area, Phase II	11,000
Total	26,191

The land areas acquired form a contiguous state ownership, starting at Cedar Creek in Double Trouble State Park and arcing to the south through the existing state-owned lands of Greenwood, Wharton, and Bass River state forests to the confluence of the Wading and Mullica rivers at Swan Bay.

At the same time, the acquisition of Cedar Creek, referred to as the last remaining major river system within the Atlantic coastal area of New Jersey almost entirely free of pollution, is considered by the DEP as having tremendous potential as a future source of potable water (as were the added headwaters of the Batsto River). With the current crisis of the 1980-81 drought throughout the Middle Atlantic States, it is not surprising that potable water systems have become the focus of preservation efforts by the state. In addition, through the preservation-area acquisition program, state recreational areas are not only preserved but enlarged considerably for such activities as camping, boating, and swimming.

How do these benefits to the state's overall water and recreational goals compensate those who view these acquisitions only as a loss of tax ratables for their community? At the moment, the counties are allowed a payment in lieu of taxes for a period of 13 years, and on a downward sliding scale. What happens as those years slip away and the costs to municipalities appear to them greater than the benefits of preserving the water and land? This question will provide the grist for new mills of conflict and concession as the issue raised at the beginning of this study is raised again and again: land and water as a resource versus land and water as a commodity.

SUMMARY

In summary, then, it is evident that the 1970-80 decade produced a significant number of bureaucratic and legislative arrangements aimed at preservation and development control of the Pine Barrens region. Both federal and state agencies were galvanized toward regulatory mechanisms that would delimit the industrial growth within the rural region. These solutions involved the collective action of citizen-based voluntary groups, congressmen, senators, state legislators, federal and state bureaucrats, the governor, and, finally, the president.

The splintering within these various categories can be mentioned only briefly in this study, but in many cases it was considerable. For example, within the Department of the Interior, initial actors in the drama, such as Jack Hauptmann in the Bureau of Outdoor Recreation, were later replaced by representatives from the Bureau of Land Management and the National Park Service. Within the state bureaucracy, the Pinelands Review Committee was staffed by the Department of Community Affairs. With the passage of the Pinelands National Reserve Act, that agency changed hands with the Department of Environmental Protection. Within the bureaucratic agencies themselves, there were competing factions jockeying for control and subsequently power in the role of land stewardship.

Control mechanisms themselves focus upon housing development as the central issue. The 1980 management plan (the New Jersey Pinelands Comprehensive Management Plan) would strictly limit construction in over 1 million acres of land; but there are other systems that escalate the market value of land without the direct use of the bulldozer. Parcels of land are currently changing hands, sold and resold at spiraling prices from owner to owner. This is happening with the mere promise of development possibilities while the land remains vacant. This action certainly compounds the task of land acquisition under mandate by federal funding. The State Department of Environmental Protection, whose role it is to locate titles and carry out acquisitions, is faced with policy decision making for the 1980s that would guide its acquisition activities.

Transportation systems themselves can provide the avenues for future development. For example, the Delaware River Port Authority is currently engaged in planning for the high-speed line traveling from Philadelphia to Berlin, New Jersey. Along the stop points the commission must decide the nature of development possible through the introduction of this system of public transportation. At the same time, the Technical Advisory Committee of the Intergovernmental Planning Program is studying the question of off-shore oil leasing for the Mid-Atlantic Region. This committee, to which this author has been named a member, is currently planning the development of an on-shore pipeline transportation system from the Baltimore Canyon. Each of these activities suggests that changes will occur in the region even as strong measures are legislated to restrict them. The decade of the 1980s will no doubt provide new acts in the drama of conflict and management policies of the New Jersey Pine Barrens.

MAP 3

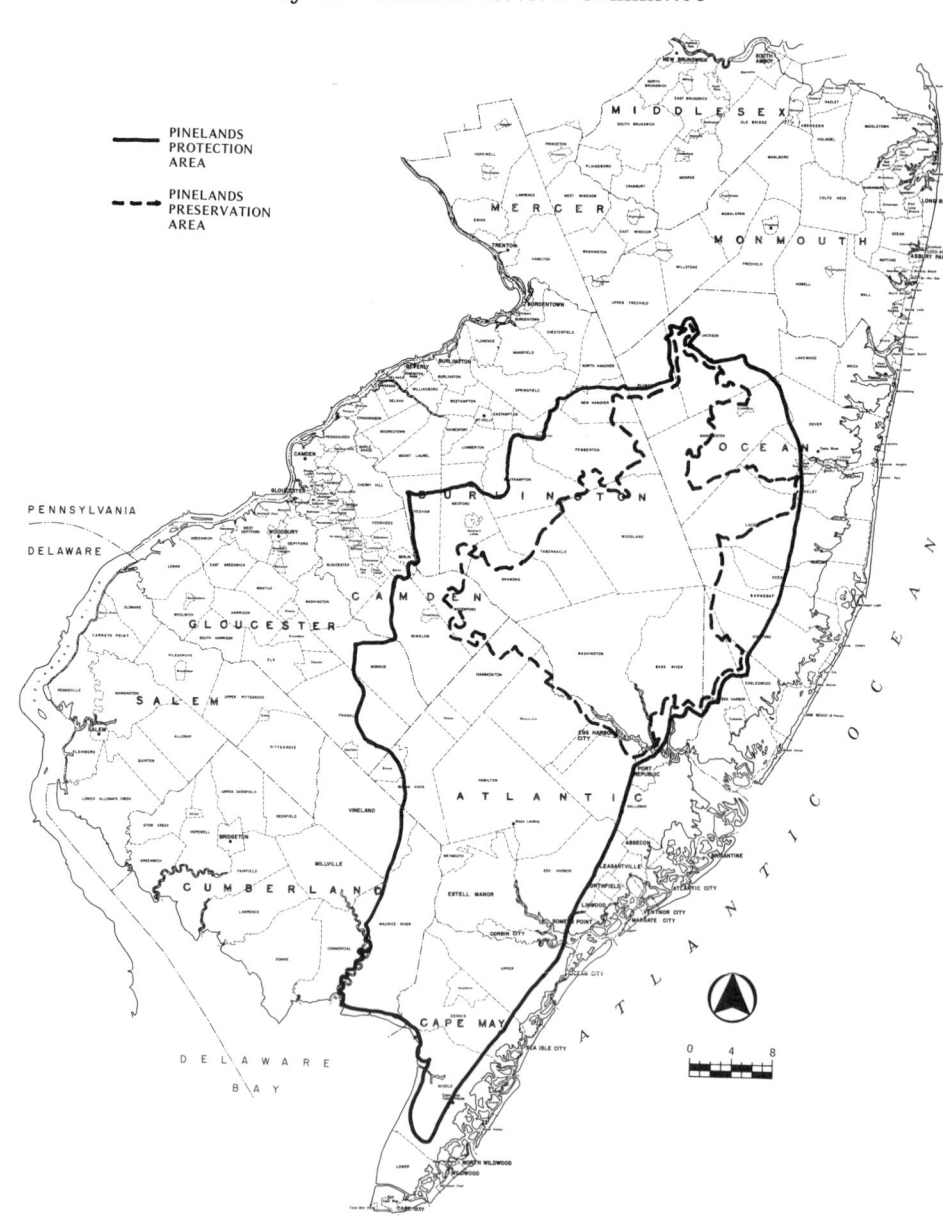

Pine Barrens Protection and Preservation Areas Designated
by the Pinelands Review Committee

Source: State of New Jersey, Governor's Pinelands Review Committee.

7

THE LAND ETHIC AND SOCIAL CHANGE

> An ethic, ecologically, is a limitation on freedom of action in the struggle for existence.
> Leopold 1966:238

This final chapter is devoted to an exploration of those social, historical, and political changes that have moved to shape the land use conflicts and public policies in the Pine Barrens during the two-decade period from the beginning of the 1960s to the early years of the 1980s.

This book has been a historic and ethnographic analysis of the social forces that shape the planning of a natural area in an urban region. The Pine Barrens has been a specific case in point; but the general aim of the research was to develop a "natural history" of planning for the preservation and use of large tracts of underdeveloped land close to centers of dense population. As such, we have sought to understand the tensions between and within groups of people who gather together as interest groups; and who pose a unique point of view on the question of how a particular tract of land and water will be used in the present and for the future.

Thus, the Pine Barrens has been the focus of study as an empirical case of natural area planning. In this exploration of the Pine Barrens, we have sought to discover principles that apply in possible future projects. The analysis, then, moves on to compare these findings with a similar, but distinct, turn of events in Canada. Hence, the findings and conclusions reached in this study of a unique region within the industrial Northeast Coast expands beyond the limitations inherent in a single case study to illuminate concepts and theories on broad-based questions of social conflict and of its implications for land use planning.

Land management public policy has a direct bearing upon the structure of social life of a region. These policies determine growth, limited or massive, of a given region and whether, to a certain extent, the economy of that society is largely agricultural or industrial. Therefore, one outcome of this research is to provide a theoretical framework through which the analysis of social impact and assessment is made understandable in terms larger than the simple elaboration on polarity of views with respect to a particular land use dispute. We move from the particular to the general, from the micro to the macro perspective. It is possible to suggest a comparison with other U.S., Canadian, and international environmental conflicts.

Finally, since conflict and social change are two major concerns of sociology as a discipline, it makes sense that the sociological perspective serves as the framework for the analysis of such a phenomenon. Therefore we begin with a sociohistorical perspective to advance the point that a change in the social and economic organization of this formerly rural region set within a larger urban context has in fact been in process.

HOW SOCIAL CHANGE IMPACTS UPON THE PINE BARRENS

We have sought to analyze several problems and perspectives emerging from the technological nondevelopment of this rural region and the countervailing forces of industrialization, urbanization, and technological advance.

Two periods—the early 1960s, referred to as the jetport controversy and the late 1960s-early 1970s, the Pinelands Environmental Council controversy—present empirical evidence of the social forces that serve to generate interest groups and interest-group formation. The generation of such groups centers on the formation of social policy with respect to the use of land and water.

In the historical perspective, for the first 300 years of U.S. settlement there was no social policy with respect to preserving land per se. There is, instead, the American concept of conquering the wilderness and "Yankee ingenuity" toward the development of industrialism. The fact that industry did not survive in the Pinelands and that the region did in fact remain a wilderness was not a result of rational social planning, environmental policies, and interest-group pressures: little if any legislation was enacted during those 300 years that would govern the use of the land and water.

Early in the twentieth century, however, by an act of the New Jersey legislature, the water supply in the Pine Barrens was preserved from an ingenious plan of the Philadelphia Whartons. However, a generalized land and water policy did not come into governmental and citizen focus until the 1960s. The policy makers generating this decision included an ever-widening circle of bureaucrats, politicians, and citizen groups.

The conflict that ensued did not represent a class struggle in the Marxian sense of proletarian and bourgeoisie (though citizen environmentalists tend to be upper and upper middle class); rather, the disputes sprang from the monopolization of resources and resource management, from long-standing U.S. policies of laissez faire in industrial development and more recent notions of social planning and conservation. This process of social planning produced administration of policy at higher levels of government bureaucracies, while political legitimization was gained through the emergence of citizen interest groups as autonomous agencies. The result is an ever-widening conflict relevant to the making of social policy.

FINDINGS

Land that was undeveloped in the most expansive phases of U.S. society remained undeveloped as long as a greater opportunity existed elsewhere. The initial phases of U.S. expansion ignored marginal land along the developed areas. Only when urbanism had reached a point where land was scarce within those developed areas did interest focus on marginal land near to or within highly developed areas. This occurred after World War II with respect to airports and later with respect to housing. Therefore, the 1960s witnessed the eruption of land use disputes first in northern New Jersey with the proposed jetport, in the region known as the Great Swamp. It was only when citizen interest-group organization mounted pressure from northern communities on the crest of political gubernatorial campaigns that the Pine Barrens, the marginal land, became the center of interest for such development.

At the time that such marginal land became of interest for economic developers, the environmental movement, whose roots had been emerging in tandem with economic development interests, had itself reached a stage of organization and development that made it possible to resist the intensive development of marginal lands in those urban environments. As an environmental resource, undeveloped areas in metropolitan regions have far more emotional appeal than undeveloped areas in distant regions. For each urban region, such areas are reminders of our own particular rural-agricultural and national inheritance.

In addition, at levels of underdevelopment, real estate developers and local commercial bodies have vested interests in the land as it remains in its undeveloped state. Local farmers and landholders in the Pine Barrens lobbied for decision-making power and resource control when they realized that preservation policies would restrict the marketing of land. Their mode of protest centered on populist ideals of local autonomy and the traditional posture of antifederalism.

In early stages of the environmental movement of the 1960s, the groups involved were Earth Movement people, upper middle class professionals, and old upper class "Yankee stock" who sentimentalized or idealized open space with all its various meanings. All were part of a national movement, and that national movement became embodied in national legislation that placed resources under the trusteeship of the Department of the Interior and with some of the regulatory state agencies. In New Jersey, the Department of Environmental Protection emerged in the 1970s as the newest state agency and the first statewide institution to regulate land and water use outside the traditional roles of agricultural and conservation agencies. As agencies of the federal and state governments assumed guardianship of the natural resources, the Earth Movement people dropped out as did some of the middle class and upper middle class individuals who were not able to sustain the zeal and interest in the absence of a specific dramatic crisis. Groups such as the Sierra Club, the Audubon Society, and the Appalachian Mountain Club, which existed long before the 1960s, were able to maintain the ongoing interest in environmental disputes.

The enactment of state and federal legislation in part became a vehicle for the institutionalization of all interest groups prior to the creation of the Pinelands Environmental Council and federal and state legislation. The interest groups had operated outside of the institutional agencies. Now they became part of the institutional machinery, yet they retained basic economic and ideological interests. Thus, the PEC was formed from the drafting of legislation by local control interests. The creation of the council as a regional planning agency was their attempt to offset the intrusion of the National Park Service as the conservation and management unit. In doing so, the PEC brought into legitimacy those actors in the land use disputes whose basic economic and ideologic interests centered on marketing the resources. Thus the specific interest group became legitimized as a regional planning agency. As the planning agency for the Pine Barrens, the leadership of local control in each group was no longer engaged in protest activities. It was no longer necessary to do so since they themselves were the "bureaucrats."

Five basic issues emerged from this study: the more inclusive character of social class participation in environmental disputes since the turn of the century; how and when marginal land becomes the focus of land use disputes; the emergence of the suburban middle class and its subsequent participation in environmental disputes; the changeover from the 1960s to the 1980s of citizen involvement, from protesters to professional planners on government commissions; and the separation of myths from realities in terms of the interdependencies of rural-urban networks, particularly in urbanized regions. These basic issues are best interpreted, first, from the broader-based milieu in which such social changes have occurred, and second, from the specific outcomes and findings in the Pine Barrens case study.

A HISTORICAL PERSPECTIVE

Beginning with the historical roots in the U.S. concern with the environment at the turn of the century, which engaged first the writers and philosophers as ideologists of moral regeneration through nature, we go on to reinterpret these events in light of expanding industrialization. The environmental movement reveals, in retrospect, the emergence of social and political policy that draws ideologies, and later a political framework, from interest groups based upon specific social classes.

The roots of the environmental movement in the United States take us back in time to the upper class "old wealth" who were, at the turn of the century, the proponents of conservation and preservation and who carried with them a tradition and image of elitism. Since World War II, industrialization has forced changes upon the open landscape and, accordingly, interest-group participation has moved downward in social class, adding the citizens of the middle classes to those voluntary associations devoted to environmental protection as well as to those who would industrialize the use of land.

As a further outcome of advancing industrialization, the decline of agriculture, and therefore the agricultural use of land, leaves in its wake the advance of suburbia. This latter use of land involves the construction of settlements and housing, a use of land that has heretofore survived as woodland and open farmland. Thus the continued advance of suburbia generates new conflicts and newer interest groups brought on by the second wave of counterindustrialization in the post-World War II "affluent society."

MODERN ENVIRONMENTAL CONFLICTS

The environmental conflicts of the 1960s were not crises of the central cities. They did not arise out of the problems of cities and poverty, the concurrent struggle for housing, schools, hospitals, and jobs; rather they were products of suburban society. They were partly the problems of the fragmented society, no longer confident about the priorities and values of unlimited growth and industrialization. At this point the environmental movement joined the forces of the upper middle classes toward the protection of their nonurban existence, the community that that embodied, and the social order inherent in that organization of life. Like the old wealth—the upper classes of the nineteenth century who actively supported the federal policies of Roosevelt and Pinchot—the new middle class would support decisions to delimit industrial growth on their home environment. Therefore, we must understand the setting of that home environment in which these policies and conflicts take place: the Northeast region known as megalopolis.

MEGALOPOLIS AS A SOCIAL SETTING

The Northeastern seaboard of the United States, the nation's first megalopolis, is a region of immense urbanized concentration within which New Jersey falls to the south of Boston and to the north of Washington, D.C.

Megalopolis emerged as a result of the growth of cities, the division of labor within civilized society, and the development of world resources. The dynamics of urbanization produced a revolution in land use, the separation between the place of work from the place of residence. In the process the old distinctions of urban and rural were blurred. Gottmann (1961:5) points out: "Every city in this region spreads out far and wide around its original nucleus; it grows amidst an irregularly colloidal mixture of rural and suburban landscapes."

Friedmann (1973) defines the concept as an "urban field" where the technology such as an efficiently managed network of freeways, electric energy, and water systems interconnects farms and forests with urban settlements. This reshaping of the land use and sprawl of the city was concomitant with the decline of older systems of agriculture. Ultimately, the ever-widening circles of growth reached formerly isolated pockets of rural settlements. Areas of open space were highly vulnerable; although they were low in population density, and therefore considered rural, their economy was no longer based upon small-scale agricultural practices. The agricultural systems of the small independent farmer had become industrialized and corporatized in the style of big business and big government. This decline of the agricultural society in the wake of the industrial society was identified by Weber at the turn of the century.

THE DECLINE OF THE AGRICULTURAL SOCIETY IN AN INDUSTRIAL SOCIETY

As early as 1904, Max Weber noted the descendent path of the European rural-agricultural society. He saw no visible distinction between rural and urban societies—everyone it seemed had become an entrepreneur:

> The constant proprietor of the soil, the landlord is not an agriculturalist. . . . The laborers are partly seasonal and migrating: the rest are journeymen of a certain time and then are scattered again. . . . If there is a specific rural social problem it is only this: Whether and how the rural community or society, which no longer exists, can arise again to be strong and enduring (Gerth and Mills 1958:363).

The manner in which the land was distributed determined the economic and political conditions of the country, and ownership of land, more precisely estates, gave legitimacy to one's status aspiration rather than aiding the development of an agricultural system. Moreover, the technical changes in agricultural production, which may have diminished the size of the labor force, were themselves limited by what Weber called the law of decreasing productivity of the land and stronger natural limits and conditions of production.

Agriculture in the new capitalist society of the early twentieth century could not offer an avenue, an ascending pathway, to the market economy. There were certain limits on the means of production. Weber was not sanguine about the future of natural resources nor the U.S. agricultural system:

> We must not forget that the boiling heat of modern capitalistic culture is connected with needless consumption of natural resources, for which there are no substitutes. It is difficult to determine how long the present supply of coal and ore will last. The utilization of new farm lands will soon have reached

> an end in America; in Europe it no longer exists. The agriculturalist can never hope to gain more than a modest equivalent for his work as a husbandman. He is, in Europe, and also to a great extent in this country, excluded from participating in the great opportunities open to speculative business talent (Gerth and Mills 1958:366).

The new industrial society had turned around the older economic order of providing work and sustenance for the greatest possible number, to providing as many crops as possible for the market with as few workers as possible. The result was the decline of rural communities, as workers migrated to the cities. What was left was the "capitalistic farmer striving for entrepreneurial profits and the landowners' interest in rents."

Weber predicted that the decline of the rural society would, in time, affect the U.S. social structure, both the increase of population density and the concurrent rise in land values. This change from agricultural societies to industrial societies, from rural settlements to urban fields, is in fact the social force underlying one set of conflicts in the Pine Barrens of southern New Jersey.

In summary, then, the development of the preservation movement at the turn of the century was a social movement to contain the impact of industrialization upon the old order and the old wealth. That industrial impact had its visible effects in the growth of cities and the expansion of the working class population.

The alliance of the preservationists and the conservationists at the turn of the century with the federal agencies was a means of gaining legitimate power over land use decisions, and this pattern of power alliance continued throughout the next 70 years as the growth of cities became the growth of suburbs.

CHANGE AND THEN CONFLICT: THE RECENT PAST

Following centuries of rural isolation, starting when English Quakers or Swedish, French, and Dutch adventurers first displaced the Leni-Lenape tribe of the Delaware Indians in the early seventeenth century, the Pine Barrens has been sporadically "discovered" and then "lost," until the post-World War II society invented suburbia as a significant way of life and technology as the means for addressing its goals.

Urban decentralization was occurring at the same time as the decline of older systems of small-scale agriculture. Therefore, throughout the Northeast coastal region, in New Jersey, Long Island, and Massachusetts, the decline of land utilized for the production of agriculture resulted in the reassessment of land toward the more profitable residential and industrial development. This process in turn enlarged the sphere of urbanization in an ever-widening ring, reaching, finally, to the marginal land within the Pine Barrens.

Abruptly, within the 20 years between 1960 and 1980, the region has been the focus of intense conflict over the management and utilization of land and water. These conflicts have been expressed in ideologies that reflect a concern for the social and environmental impact of urbanization and suburbanization upon small-scale rural life styles and the natural area in which they coexist. The problem, however, is more complex than the single polarity between the folk life and the city life. While local agriculturists lament in populist ideologies the passing of the "frontier," and of the yeoman-farmer, they are in fact participating in the corporate organization of what has now become a national network of agribusiness. Farmers as businessmen have learned that their land, rather than the agricultural product they have for so long been cultivating, is the real commodity.

On the other hand, those environmentalists who reflect upon preservationist values are participating in that same corporate society. Only the Pineys, the woods people, have remained outside the urban field.

This ideal portrait of our earlier preindustrial system of social organization forms part of each of the opposing groups' rationales for beliefs and political actions. It is the social action that springs from this pastoral ideology that marks the groups as polarized; while one lobbies for controlled growth, the other supports unlimited growth.

It is the interaction between urban growth and agricultural decline that sets the stage for conflicts between the proponents of localism (which is management of the resources on an informal arrangement) and those of federalism as a system of social organization. The tension exists because cities and suburbs expand, but the impact is set into motion because technology has placed limits upon the amount of land necessary for agricultural production. This gap between the agricultural system and the industrial system is shortened when housing or other forms of industrial uses provide a more profitable use of open space than does agricultural production.

Now, we may ask, which theoretical construct provides a framework for interpreting this analysis? First, it is necessary to identify the problem of being one of social change, and, second, to understand the impact of that change upon the social organization. Clearly, Ferdinand Toennies' ideal-type models of social organization, as they are analyzed in "Community and Society: Gemeinschaft and Gesellschaft" (1964), seem relevant to this discussion.

THEORETICAL PERSPECTIVES

In the style of Max Weber, Toennies constructed ideal-type models of social organization. They were not intended to mirror reality since they were constructed in black and white, in terms of polarity and striking contrasts.

Within Toennies' ideal-type concepts of social organization, the Gemeinschaft defines a life style characterized by the rural folk life in which the center of social organization is local. The family, the church, and the town constitute the controlling agents of the society. Moreover, the agricultural economy is tied to the past and to unwritten but powerful mores. In contrast, the Gesellschaft depicts the organization of city life in which the real controlling agent is the state; controls are generated by written legislation rather than unwritten folk traditions. This was the system that Weber viewed (more optimistically than Toennies) as the rational-legal system.

While Toennies viewed these two systems of social organization as dichotomous, he made note of the enveloping power of the national-legal system upon the folk-rural tradition. He considered this form of social change as a force that was destructive in nature and direction. Thus he noted that the entire culture had been transformed into a civilization of state and Gesellschaft. Surely this, he proclaimed, was the doom of culture.

Though Toennies described the tensions between two distinct systems, it must be remembered that he was constructing an ideal-type of model for purposes of analysis. The application of this polarized system, that is, between Gemeinschaft and Gesellschaft, with the merging rural and urban systems can carry us only part way in our understanding of this social change. Of greater value is identifying where the poles have in fact interconnected: where urban life and rural life have exchanged and merged into a system of interdependency. For example, the tension between rural small towns and the urbanized mass society reported by Vidich and Bensman (1968) in the early 1960s resulted from ambivalence on the part of small-town people. While they resented and mistrusted the urban system, they nurtured some admiration for the cosmopolitan life and, more importantly, the power of the national system, a system that excluded them.

Only ten years later, this author's study of conflicts and change in the Pine Barrens depicts a rural community whose leaders at least have become part of the national corporate system, and whose political networks no longer stop at the county seat.

CITIZENS JOIN THE BUREAUCRACY: THE NEW ERA OF LAND PLANNING COMMISSIONS

From the beginning of the 1970s, government in the state of New Jersey has enacted legislation that legitimized land planning commissions, and some of this legislation has focused on the Pine Barrens.

At the state level, Governor Brendan Byrne named a cabinet-level, citizen-based planning committee, a committee to which this author was subsequently appointed and whose purpose was to represent statewide interests in the Pine Barrens. The Pinelands Review Committee, as it was called, was charged with establishing boundaries for the protection and preservation of the region and making recommendations for future management systems. Appointments to the PRC, unlike its predecessor, the Pinelands Environmental Council, were to reflect a wide spectrum of interests and geographic locations. More importantly, the 17 members were citizens outside of government employ, purported to represent the interests of environmentalists and builders alike. A state planning entity from the Department of Community Affairs, and to a lesser extent from the Department of Environmental Protection, were assigned as staff to the PRC. This arrangement is a striking departure from planning in the 1960s when only professional government planners were involved, and where the public would serve as critic from the sidelines.

Other legislative concepts fostered similar concepts of citizen-based planning commissions: Congressman Florio's Green Line Boundaries proposal in the House of Representatives; a similar bill introduced later by Congressmen Hughes and Forsythe; and finally, the successful effort by Senator Harrison Williams in tandem with departing senior Senator Clifford Case that resulted in legislation passed as part of the Omnibus Parks Bill.

Each of these legislative plans calls for citizen-based planning commissions, unique to New Jersey needs, but not unlike the direction taken by New York State in its Adirondack Park Commission, nor Vermont in its creation of the Regional Plan Commissions in the early 1970s. From the 1970s onward, in fact, the management of scenic or natural areas adjacent to urban regions in the eastern strip of megalopolis has been the subject of land planning disputes that have ended (temporarily) with the establishment of citizen-based land planning agencies or commissions. As such, member-planners eventually develop the experience and sophistication to work with the highly subtle form of power maneuvering through which interest groups attempt to control land management policies. For example, as of November 1978, when President Carter signed into act the Pinelands National Reserve Section of the National Parks and Recreation Act of 1978 (which included the Williams bill), local leaders of the agricultural community in the Pine Barrens have argued for a greater local representation on the designated land planning commission; and to that end they have been successful. Written into the act were 7 of the 15 commissioners to be appointed by local freeholders of the counties so designated. Environmental organizations have lobbied as well for their part of the commission.

Not only have local spokesmen lobbied in Washington over the casting of commissions, they have testified at congressional subcommittee hearings on Congressman Florio's bill, the Pinelands National Ecological Reserve; and on Hughes and Forsythe's bill, the Pinelands National Wildlife Refuge (all of the above-named bills emerged finally through the Senate under the aegis of Senator Williams).

This participation in the power system of the national structure illustrates a greater interconnection between the local organization and the state. Not only are the citizens critics of the national and state governments, they are manipulators of that power as well. Thus the vocal, more powerful representatives of public interest groups, through their participation in planning commissions, become the architects of social impact as well as the recipients of whatever costs or benefits those policies promote.

COMPARISONS WITH CANADIAN ENVIRONMENTAL DECISION MAKING

When the mayor of Toronto, Ontario, John Sewell, had written his analysis of urban growth problems in this Canadian province in 1977, he was then alderman, and his depiction of the problem was one of unchecked growth from cities to the surrounding countryside.

On the surface, at least, Toronto and the surrounding Ontario countryside mirrors the urban-rural setting within which the Pine Barrens rests. The city is a cosmopolitan center with a population of several million, while only 18 miles beyond is the hilly and beautifully wooded setting for Maple, Ontario. With its class-one agricultural land, its many ponds and streams, the region is largely open space and farmland, dairy farms, and small private homes for people who choose to live outside the city. It is a portrait of a setting that in time and character resembles the countrified suburbia of the Great Swamp controversy noted in Chapter 4. What brought threat to and action from this community was not the idea of a jetport, as was the case for the Great Swamp, but the proposed contract for the largest garbage dump in North America hewed out of an old gravel pit. Accordingly, citizens and residents saw the operation as a threat to hydrogeologic resources, as the location of the site coincided with the headwaters of the Don River and stood to contaminate the water supply of the region.

Up to this point we have a comparable case for study with the outcome of the Pine Barrens chronicle, with certain significant exceptions. While New Jersey citizens banded together in the 1960s to form protest groups, and significantly formalized themselves further in the 1970s to enter the halls of government as planners-commissioners, in 1976 the Canadians of Maple, lacking an existing citizen organization, chose to protest on a farm-by-farm basis by testifying before an environmental hearing board for a tortuous year-long period and at some expense.

What these citizens learned, somewhat to their surprise—as did the local garden clubs of the Pine Barrens—was that the long-stable government of Ontario was unresponsive to their phone calls and to their desire to influence the outcome of environmental decisions. Or more surprising, in one instance, a Maple homeowner pointed out that she had to subpoena a government bureaucrat in order to force him to see her.

This sense of powerlessness and separation from the governmental decision-making process also has been expressed by Canadians from the Province of Alberta, when Cold Lake farmers and reservation Indians found themselves faced with the prospect of a $4.7 billion heavy oil plant in their home environment.

Farmers from Alberta referred to their independent life as one they coveted, as did the earlier farmers in the Pine Barrens; but this led to their lack of formal organization to deal with the powerful energy interests who influence government decisions on land use. Further, they expressed anger and disbelief at the idea that government officials did not represent them or their interests.

In an interview with Tom Turner, a farmer who is leading the movement to preserve his land, an Alberta newspaper reports: "They attend hearings to discuss the impact of the projects, armed only with rough briefs drawn up in their spare time, yet they face a barrage of oil company and government lawyers who pull volumes of statistics from their briefcases" (Alberta Sunday Tab, December 3, 1978).

The Indians from the Cold Lake Indian Reserve object to this change in the use of land because of the impact it may have upon their life style. One man, Marcel Piche, commented that despite offers of compensation and jobs in the oil industry for Reserve

Indians, they would lose the important activities of hunting and fishing, and that these economies and cultural systems were directly downgraded in the 1950s when the government opened up the Primrose bombing range in the area where they lived. This last point brings to mind the threat of a tank-training range proposed by the military in the Pine Barrens in the mid-1960s.

Finally, this discussion suggests the Wilson (1973) study of the Rip Van Winkle Valley, the Arrow Lakes region of British Columbia. Here local independence and isolation labeled the area and the people "the Ozarks of Canada." In a portrait of agricultural isolation, we note resemblances to the Pineys. They were a land and a people forgotten in time until the British Columbia Hydro and Power Authority proposed to build a dam there. Much like the Pine Barrens agricultural landholders, the people of the Arrow Lakes region viewed compensation as a prime issue. Thus Wilson (1973: 146) concludes: "The evidence suggests that the whole Arrow Lakes problem as seen by the people affected was overshadowed by the question of compensation."

Here, the resemblances of Canadian and Pine Barrens case studies depart, despite the similarities of issues; for even in the 1980s it does not seem plausible for these Canadians to lobby for participation on planning commissions. This separation between government planning and citizen involvement on land and water resource policies is still clearly drawn in the Canadian arena. For example, one activist commented to this author on the Maple, Ontario, scene: "I don't know how you go about putting people on boards."

Though the Maple residents have won their battle, momentarily, with the garbage dump issue, they have begun to face new issues with respect to the use of their open space, and they have also begun to develop some sophistication with the notion of community participation. For example, the residents of the Maple countryside have begun to build an organization to deal with environmental conflicts. More importantly, the composition of the group departs from the isolated local scene and draws representation from an international organization, the Sierra Club. This change in interest group composition reminds us of the change in the mid-1970s in Pine Barrens communities, from local watershed associations to joining with Sierra Club political sophistication. However, the Ontario citizens are still protesting decisions from outside the halls of government, in a manner familiar to the Pine Barrens and Great Swamp residents of the early 1960s.

Part of this difference between the two countries with respect to public participation can be explained by the more conservative model for behavior in public arenas by English-based Canadians.

One woman commented: "Canadians are terribly nervous of anybody who stands up—they don't like Ralph Nader or anything like that."

Perhaps more basic to the difference between U.S. and Canadian modes of environmental conflicts and decision making is the relative absence of social unrest in the latter country's modern history, an unrest that marked the U.S. social landscape and character for more than a decade.

In New Jersey, for example, citizen activism in cities such as Newark, Plainfield, and Camden in the decade of the 1960s brought about turmoil and instability for citizens of urban and suburban communities. One of the outcomes of that era, at least with respect to social change, was the breakdown of distance between citizen and government. Community participation was a concept that took precedence in the drafting of legislative plans for health care and later environmental planning, though certainly the tension between government and the citizen sector was not to be overlooked. The selection of appointments to task forces and planning committees tended to neutralize the more outspoken leadership of community or minority representation.

On the other hand, the more stable system in Canadian government over the past two decades provides minimal experience with the U.S. ideology of pluralism and public participation; this difference in national character and experience sets the stage for citizen and government behavior in the process of environmental decision making. We cannot say that one is better than the other; we can only note the similarity of issues, the differences in modes of solutions, and, finally that the intricacies of these differences can contribute to the overall form and content of environmental decision making.

NEW SYSTEMS OF GOVERNMENT STEWARDSHIP

Another significant change in the involvement of government in land and water management is the shift from the national parks concept that has been so pervasive in Western land management systems. Open space in proximity to urban and suburban development brings forth powerful resistance from those communities surrounding the area. They resist the idea of outside management systems that cut off the possibilities of any form of growth or development for that region. The compromise reached in the Pine Barrens solution was that of a state/federal partnership in which the open space is managed by an appointed commission. Under this system, the federal government provides the funding for planning and acquisition of sensitive lands, but the state government maintains the lion's share of power and control. It is the state government, and more particularly the governor, that selects and appoints that commission; and it is the state agency that identifies those parcels of land for acquisition. Therefore, while the new system of federal/state partnership replaces the sealed solutions of the national park concept, it allows for the renegotiation of commission appointees and acquisition policies that would reflect a change in the elected state administrations. The viability of the new Pine Barrens land and water management plan will be tested during the early years of the 1980s—in 1981, in fact, when an election year will provide a new governor and new administrative policies.

CONCLUSIONS: THE GREAT LAND TRANSFORMATION

Polanyi (1944:178) points out that "what we call land is an element of nature inextricably interwoven with man's institutions. To isolate it and form a market out of it was perhaps the weirdest of all undertakings of our ancestors." To separate land from people and organize society as a means of satisfying the real-estate market was part of the concept of the market economy, and the growth of the market economy had ramifications for human societies as well as the condition of open space.

Land has become a market commodity, and the old system of agriculture that provided only for maintaining subsistence levels of independence and even isolation has become commercialized into ever larger agribusinesses.

To change the market system of land is to change the structure of society as well, as both are closely related. To change land as a commodity back to land as a resource, without shifting the rules and structures of the market society, would indeed be virtually impossible. Any attempt produces conflict. At another level, changing the market position of land could eventually lead to changes in the structure of society, and this change may well be in process.

Land use planning in urban regions has since the late 1960s involved higher and higher levels of government authority and the jurisdiction of federal power is in this area attacked by the "rugged individualists" as a denial of freedom. Such attacks are similar to earlier attacks on federal intervention regulating free enterprise. Comments Polanyi (1944:257):

> Planning and control are being attacked as a denial of freedom. Free enterprise and private ownership are declared to be essentials of freedom. . . . The

> freedom that regulation creates is denounced as unfreedom . . . the U.S.S.R. which used planning, regulation and control as its instruments, has not yet put the liberties promised in her Constitution into practice, and probably, the critics add, never will. . . . But to turn against regulation means to turn against reform.

The reform Polanyi refers to is the planning of society toward the regulation and control of powerful and independent trusts and monopolies.

Land use disputes are another test of the political and economic autonomy of the market economy. The struggle goes to the very roots of industrial-capitalist society and cannot be seen simply as the contest of the forces of commodity versus resource.

Those who support the idea of land as a resource, the environmentalists and conservationists, are also practicing and interacting within the market system. The drive for change is not a holistic move. Nevertheless, the politicization of the environmental movements has shifted the planning power toward higher levels of state and federal bureaucracies and away from local landholders, thereby, in effect, creating national controls over land use and open space as a means of preserving it.

APPENDIX

This case study is not a specific technique. It is a way of organizing social data so as to preserve the unitary character of the social object being studied. It is a holistic view that may focus upon a person, a family or other social group, a set of relationships or processes, or even an entire culture.

Despite the difference in the unit of organization under study, each case must deal with a number of common methodological considerations: What is the problem under examination? On what basis is the unit chosen for examination? What method(s) will be used to gather the necessary data? What variables are to be considered? How are the respondents for the study selected?

COMMUNITY STUDY ON A REGIONAL SCALE

In its broadest sense, this study is a community analysis, although the parameters are regional and as such encompass 34 municipalities (or townships), part of four New Jersey counties, and a minimum of 350,000 acres, within which are four state forests. The problem under examination—What is the fate of large tracts of remaining open space in densely populated urban agglomerations?—is analyzed within the framework of planning. The study is a historic and ethnographic analysis of the social forces that shape the planning of a natural area in an urban region.

SELECTION OF A REGION FOR STUDY

The northeast megalopolis region, the area south of Boston and north of Washington, D.C., has within it the most urbanized concentration of population density, interconnecting networks of major metropolitan regions, and counterforces of rural, open space. Three centuries ago, this powerful concentration of people and activities was a wilderness. Yet only within the past two decades (since the early 1960s) has land use planning and the preservation of open spaces been a subject of social and political dispute.

Within the state of New Jersey, three major open-space land areas have been the subject of considerable debate: the Pine Barrens, the Delaware Water Gap, and Sandy Hook National Park.

Based on an earlier study of Sandy Hook (Goldstein 1975), the author explored the considerations of planning for a parcel of land already removed from the commodity market, one that had become a national park, and noted that interest-group formation continued to generate planning decisions at higher levels of bureaucratic structure. Concurrently, the Delaware Water Gap decision to bar the Army Corps of Engineers' plan for the building of a dam laid to rest, temporarily, the intense Delaware Water Gap dispute.

Therefore, only the Pine Barrens remained as a tract of open space whose fate had not been decided. Between 1975 and 1980, the Pine Barrens became the focus of public hearings, debates, interest-group formation, and the campaign platform for New Jersey legislators and gubernatorial candidates. It was therefore possible to study the planning process while it was in fact occurring. It was for this reason that the Pine Barrens became not only appropriate as a case study but ideal.

DESCRIPTION OF THE PINE BARRENS

The New Jersey Pine Barrens occupies about 2,000 square miles (some 1,164,000 acres) of the Atlantic Coastal Plain in southeastern New Jersey. Only 25 miles from Philadelphia and 40 miles from New York City, the region is largely rural, with few settlements. Although 34 incorporated townships dot the landscape, some contain villages with populations of less than 1,000 and a main street with little more than a gas station and a grocery store. Economically, there is neither industrial development nor upland agricultural development.

Land that is owned by the federal government includes: Fort Dix Military Reservation, McGuire Air Force Base, and Lakehurst Naval Air Station. Within the Pine Barrens, 207,000 acres are federally owned. The New Jersey state government owns 162,000 acres of land in the region, which is used for recreation and water conservation.

Only the sprouting of senior citizen communities, such as leisure villages, have shifted the population composition and density and, in the process, narrowed the remaining portions of open space.

CHOICE OF METHOD: PARTICIPANT OBSERVATION, HISTORICAL ANALYSIS, AND QUANTITATIVE DATA

At the beginning of the study, relevant individuals and groups were identified through attendance at public involvement meetings.

By observing parties who participated in the dispute, I began to sort out and identify interest groups and the ideology that served as the foundation of their relative position. I introduced myself informally to those whom I wished to interview as relevant to an interest-group position. In all cases I made appointments to interview them on their home territory, either at their farm, home, or office, so that the total environment could be part of the observation.

Initially, I had hoped to cover several interviews in one day as a means of minimizing my travel; but that worked only with the Pine Coners, the group of Pineys who gave country music concerts in the region. I would attend one of their fests in an open park and draw one aside at a time, by a stream or in the woods, and tape an interview while they were not playing their banjo or fiddle. Many of the tapes of that group appropriately have music in the background.

Since the Pineys are not active nor do they participate in the planning disputes, they were sought out more as a significant part of the human settlements. I was seldom to meet one at a meeting on the Pine Barrens. For the local people in general, I found rather quickly that I would need to spend one full visiting day with the individual with whom I had sought the interview. This would invariably include a drive or walk around the sections of the Pine Barrens they were most interested in showing: their cranberry farm, the woods; the trail of "for sale" signs along sandy, desolate roads; a stream and section of woodland marked for development. Hospitality extended to the sharing of a meal, lunch at a farm, dinner on Sunday with the family.

After the second visit to an individual or family, I was told to consider myself "one of the family" and to call and come back anytime. It is at this point that remaining an uncommitted participant-observer became more difficult to sustain. With the ease of casual contacts, people began to want more of me—they not only wanted to tell me what they knew, they wanted to know what I knew. Could or should I become an information intermediary?

I decided that information that was public, but possibly unknown to that individual, would be appropriate to relay; but private thoughts and confidentiality were carefully observed. I also had to let people know that I was talking to all "sides" in the dispute. The region is not so populated nor the parties unknown to each other that anonymity is as possible in the Pine Barrens as in New York City.

Secondly, I had become known to the interest groups at all levels. I received phone calls from reporters from two major New Jersey papers looking for material on a story after, they informed me, the attorney general's office had told them that I knew more about the Pine Barrens than anyone else.

I identified three major levels of interest-group involvement: local, state, and national. Interviews were conducted at all three levels with attention paid to the deviant cases, particularly at the local level. A fourth level, independent environmental organizations, was included in the interview schedule.

On the state and national levels, I interviewed government figures, bureaucrats who took visible roles in relation to planning, and it was therefore necessary to interview several directors of divisions, deputy commissioners, and so on, to make certain that the agency position was being articulated consistently.

When I attended large public hearings, such as the Governor's Conference on the Pine Barrens (December 17, 1976), I would check on my interview coverage to see how many of those who attended were known to me and had been interviewed. Of those meetings I was unable to attend, such as Congressmen Forsythe and Hughes' conference at Cape May, I asked for and received from Congressman Forsythe's office the entire tapes of that day. Again, I double checked the relevant parties and spokespersons.

A separate set of interviews centered on reporting of past events—more particularly, the jetport controversy of the 1960s. Through the courtesy of former Governor Richard Hughes, I was able to interview his recommended source on the subject, former Commissioner of Transportation Goldberg.

Through the cooperation of Goldberg and many others, I was to locate and conduct a content analysis of planning documents and legislation pertaining to prior and current decisions. Up to this point, there had been no studies written on the political or social disputes in the Pine Barrens. This required that research be done on the primary level, with the exception of some historical work on the early history of South Jersey, which concluded with World War I. These were augmented with old Trenton State Library newspaper files and the helpful loan of personal files from the Sierra Club and radio journalist Dick Standish.

Census tract data obtained from the State Library served as the basis of population data on nineteenth-century Pine Barrens communities.

There was excellent rapport with most of the relevant parties. It was not unusual to receive phone calls from one or two individuals in an evening informing me of a meeting I might not know about that they hoped or thought I might attend, or urging me to testify for a particular issue. I refrained from testifying or making public any views, however, since I did not wish to appear partisan and lose my open access to other groups.

In addition, the sociological method was effective. In looking for the holistic view, I was able to grasp the complexity of the problem. The analysis at this point suggested that there were no simple answers, nor were there, as in the old westerns, clearly "good guys" and "bad guys." Although I did not agree with all the positions taken, I was able to understand each point of view and why it had been necessary to the group involved.

During the six years of my research activities and authorship of this book, I was to become involved in a number of projects connected with the Pine Barrens. Besides being appointed by Governor Byrne to the Pinelands Review Committee, I was a professional consultant to a television documentary film on Joe Alberts Fox Hunt and other stories of the Pine Barrens with the Global Village filmmaking team of Julie Gustafson and John Riley.

As the history and the future of the Pine Barrens continue to respond to social and political changes, so my interest and involvement with the region and the people will, no doubt, continue for many years to come.

BIBLIOGRAPHY

BOOKS AND ARTICLES

Atkinson, Brooks. 1967. Great Swamp Is Good for Nothing—But Life, Knowledge, Peace and Hope. New York Times Magazine, February 12, pp. 33-40.

Barber, John W., and Howe, Henry. 1853. Historical Collections of the State of New Jersey. Newark, N.J.: Benjamin Olds for Justus H. Bradley.

Beck, Henry Charlton. 1961. Forgotten Towns of Southern New Jersey. New Brunswick, N.J.: Rutgers University Press.

_____. 1963a. Jersey Genesis. New Brunswick, N.J.: Rutgers University Press.

_____. 1963b. More Forgotten Towns of Southern New Jersey. New York: E. P. Dutton.

Bensman, Joseph, and Vidich, Arthur J. 1971. The New American Society. Chicago: Quadrangle Books.

Bensman, Joseph, and Lilienfeld, Robert. 1973. Craft and Consciousness. New York: John Wiley.

Blackman, Leah. 1963. History of Little Egge Harbor Township, Burlington County, New Jersey. Tuckerton, N.J.: The Great John Mathis Foundation.

Bosselman, Fred, and Callies, David. 1971. The Quiet Revolution in Land Use Control. Prepared for the Council on Environmental Quality. Washington, D.C.: U.S. Government Printing Office.

Carter, Luther J. 1974. The Florida Experience. Baltimore: Johns Hopkins University Press.

Cawley, James, and Cawley, Margaret. 1971. Exploring the Little Rivers of New Jersey. New Brunswick, N.J.: Rutgers University Press.

Commoner, Barry. 1971. The Closing Circle. New York: Alfred A. Knopf.

Cooper, James Fenimore. 1823. The Leather Stocking Tales.

Crissey, Marie S. 1977. "The People of the Pines: A Description of a Group in Isolation." Unpublished paper before the New Jersey Historical Society Conference, November 5.

Dahrendorf, Ralf. 1959. Class and Class Conflict in an Industrial Society. Stanford, Calif.: Stanford University Press.

———. 1964. "Towards a Theory of Social Conflict." In Social Changes, ed. Amitai Etzioni and Eva Etzioni. New York: Basic Books.

Darling, Fraser F., and Milton, John P. 1966. Future Environments of North America. Garden City, N.Y.: Natural History Press.

Dickey, James. 1970. Deliverance. New York: Dell.

Edney, Julien J. 1976. "Human Territories Comment on Functional Properties." Environment and Behavior 8:31-47.

Fava, Sylvia F. 1975. "Beyond Suburbia." Annals of American Academy of Political and Social Science 22:10-24.

Feiveson, Harold A.; Sinden, Frank; and Socolow, Robert, eds. 1976. Boundaries of Analysis. Cambridge, Mass.: Ballinger.

Firey, Walter. 1960. Man, Mind and Environment: A Theory of Resource Use. Glencoe, Ill.: The Free Press.

Foerster, Norman, ed. 1947. American Poetry and Prose. Boston: Houghton Mifflin.

Fowler, Michale, and Herbert, William A. 1976. Harrisville: Papertown of the Pine Barrens. Eatontown, N.J.: Snell Graphics and Environmental Education Publishing Service.

Frederick, Duke; Howenstine, William L.; and Sochen, June. 1972. Destroy to Create: Interaction with the Natural Environment in the Building of America. Hinsdale, Ill.: The Dryden Press.

BIBLIOGRAPHY / 161

Friedmann, John. 1973. The Future of the Urban Habitat in Environment: A New Focus for Land-Use Planning. Washington, D.C.: National Science Foundation, pp. 57-58.

Galbraith, John Kenneth. 1967. The New Industrial State. New York: Signet.

_____. 1969. The Affluent Society. Boston: Houghton Mifflin.

Gerth, Hans H., and Mills, C. Wright. 1958. From Max Weber: Essays in Sociology. New York: Oxford University Press.

Glaser, Barney G., and Strauss, Anselm L. 1967. The Discovery of Grounded Theory: Strategies for Qualitative Research. Chicago: Aldine.

Goddard, Henry Herbert. 1913. The Kallikak Family. New York: Macmillan.

Goldstein, Joan. 1975. Sandy Hook National Park. Prepared for Gateway National Park Service, Graduate Center, City University of New York.

_____. 1977. "The Feds Are Coming. The Feds Are Coming." Meetings of the Society for the Study of Social Problems, Chicago.

_____. 1979a. "Housing Issues in Rural Communities." Rural Planning Program, April.

_____. 1979b. "The Impact of Urban Development on the Pine Barrens." Unpublished paper, International Conference on Marginal Regions, Dublin, Ireland, August.

_____. 1981. "The Pine Barrens: A Case Study of the Social Impact of Urban Development upon Rural Communities." In Social Impact Assessment: Methods, Theories and Practise, ed. Frank Testa and William Mykes. Calgary: Detselig Enterprises.

Goldstein, Joan, and Baxter P. 1977. "Pine Barrens under Pressure." Parks and Recreation, October:21-50.

Gottmann, Jean. 1961. Megalopolis. Cambridge, Mass.: M.I.T. Press.

Greenblatt, Bernard. 1971. Responsibility for Child Care. San Francisco: Jossey-Bass.

Guseman, Patricia Knight, and Hall, Judith. 1977. "Local Leader and Citizen Involvement in Assessing Technological Projects with Social Consequences." Meetings of the Society for the Study of Social Problems, Chicago.

Haefele, Edwin T., ed. 1974. The Governance of Common Property Resources. Baltimore: Johns Hopkins University Press.

Halpert, Herbert. 1947. "Folktales and Legends from the New Jersey Pine Barrens: A Collection and a Study." Ph.D. dissertation, Indiana University.

Hays, Samuel P. 1972. Conservation and the Gospel of Efficiency: The Progressive Conservation Movement 1890-1920. New York: Atheneum.

Heston, Alfred Miller, ed. 1924. South Jersey, A History, 1664-1924. New York: Lewis Historical Publishing Company.

Horowitz, Irving L. 1972. "The Environmental Cleavage: Social Ecology versus Political Economy." Social Theory and Practice 2, no. 1:125-34.

Huth, Hans. 1957. Nature and America: Three Centuries of Changing Attitudes. Berkeley: University of California Press.

Jarrett, Henry. 1958. Perspective on Conservation. Baltimore: Johns Hopkins University Press.

Kamin, Leon J. 1974. "Heredity, Intelligence, Politics, and Psychology." Eastern Psychological Association. Washington, D.C. May.

Klausner, Samuel Z. 1971. On Man and His Environment. San Francisco: Jossey-Bass.

Kobbe, Gustav. 1889. The New Jersey Coast and Pines. Short Hills, N.J.: G. Kobbe.

Kolesar, John, and Scholl, Jay. 1975a. "A Plan to Save Our Disappearing Farmland." Public Issues 4:1-5.

_____. 1975b. Saving Farmland. Princeton, N.J.: The Center for Analysis of Public Issues, March.

Kornblum, William. 1974. Blue Collar Community. Chicago: University of Chicago Press.

Leopold, Aldo. 1966. A Sand County Almanac. New York: Sierra Club/Ballantine Books.

Little, Silas. 1974. "Wildflowers of the Pine Barrens and Their Niche Requirements." New Jersey Outdoors 1.

_____. 1976. The Pine Barrens of New Jersey. October 12.

Luke, George W. 1976. Actively Devoted . . . The First Decade of the New Jersey Farmland Assessment Act. Prepared for the New Jersey Farmland Evaluation Advisory Committee, Trenton.

Lynd, Robert S., and Lynd, Helen Merrell. 1929. Middletown. New York: Harcourt, Brace and World.

Mannheim, Karl. 1940. Man and Society in an Age of Reconstruction. New York: Harcourt, Brace and World.

Marsh, George Perkins. 1864. Man and Nature. New York: Scribners.

Marx, Leo. 1964. The Machine in the Garden. New York: Oxford University Press.

McCarthy, J. S., and Zald, M. N. 1973. The Trend of Social Movements in America: Professionalism and Resource Mobilization. Morristown, N.J.: General Learning Press.

McCormick, Jack. 1970. The Pine Barrens: A Preliminary Ecological Inventory. Trenton, N.J.: New Jersey Museum.

McEvoy, James III. 1972. "The American Concern for the Environment." In Social Behavior, Natural Resources, and the Environment, ed. William Burch, Jr., Neil Cheek, and L. Taylor. New York: Harper and Row, pp. 214-36.

McMahon, William. 1973. South Jersey Towns. New Brunswick, N.J.: Rutgers University Press.

McPhee, John. 1967. The Pine Barrens. New York: Ballantine Books.

Meadows, Dennis L. 1972. *The Limits to Growth*. New York: Universe Books.

Miller, Pauline S. 1971. *Pictorial Album of Toms River, New Jersey*. Ocean County Historical Society.

Moore, Harvey. 1943. *An Old Jersey Furnace*. Baltimore: Newth-Morris Printing Co.

Morrison, Denton E. 1973. "The Environmental Movement: Conflict Dynamics." *Journal of Voluntary Action Research* 2, no. 2:74-85.

Morrison, Denton E.; Hornback, K.; and Warner, W. K. 1972. "The Environmental Movement: Some Preliminary Observations and Predictions." In *Social Behavior, Natural Resources and the Environment*, ed. William R. Burch, Jr., Neil Cheek, and L. Taylor. New York: Harper and Row, pp. 259-79.

Nash, Roderick, ed. 1968. *The American Environment: Readings in the History of Conservation*. Reading, Mass.: Addison-Wesley.

_____. 1972. *Environment and Americans*. New York: Holt, Rinehart and Winston.

_____. 1973. *Wilderness and the American Mind*. New Haven, Conn.: Yale University Press.

Pierce, Arthur D. 1957. *Iron in the Pines*. New Brunswick, N.J.: Rutgers University Press.

Polanyi, Karl. 1944. *The Great Transformation*. New York: Rinehart and Co.

Reilly, William, ed. 1973. *The Use of Land: A Citizen's Policy Guide to Urban Growth*. Task Force Report Sponsored by the Rockefeller Brothers Fund. New York: Thomas Crowell.

Schnaiberg, Allen. 1973. "Politics, Participation and Pollution: The Environmental Movement." In *Cities in Change: Studies on the Urban Condition*, ed. J. Walton and E. E. Carns. Boston: Allyn and Bacon, pp. 605-27.

Schriver, L. 1977. "Leopold's Land Ethic: Wishful Thinking or Workable Dream?" *Sierra Club Bulletin*, March, pp. 9-16.

Sewell, John. 1977. "The Suburbs." City Magazine 2.

Sills, David L. 1975. "The Environmental Movement and Its Critics." Human Ecology 3:1-41.

Stein, C. S. 1957. Towards New Towns for America. Cambridge, Mass.: M.I.T. Press.

Strong, Douglas H. 1977. "The Sierra Club: A History." Sierra 62:8.

Testa, Frank, and Mykes, William, eds. Social Impact Assessment: Methods, Theories and Practise. Calgary: Detselig Enterprises.

Thomson, Irene Taviss. 1976. "The Tocks Island Dam Controversy." In When Values Conflict—Essays on Environmental Analysis, ed. Lawrence Tribe, Sorrine S. Schelling, and John Voss. Cambridge, Mass.: Ballinger.

Thompson, Charles, Jr. 1974. Cranberry Growing. n.p.

Thoreau, Henry David. 1927. Walden. In The Heart of Thoreau's Journals, ed. Odell Shepard.

Toennies, Ferdinand. 1964. "Community and Society: Gemeinschaft and Gesellschaft." In Social Change, ed. Amitai Etzioni and Eva Etzioni. New York: Basic Books.

Tribe, Lawrence; Schelling, Sorrine S.; and Voss, John, eds. When Values Conflict—Essays on Environmental Analysis. Cambridge, Mass.: Ballinger.

Vayda, Andrew P., ed. 1969. Environment and Cultural Behavior. Garden City, N.Y.: Natural History Press.

Vidich, Arthur J., and Bensman, Joseph. 1968. Small Towns in Mass Society. Princeton, N.J.: Princeton University Press.

Whyte, William H. 1968. The Last Landscape. New York: Doubleday.

Wilson, J. W. 1973. People in the Way. Toronto: University of Toronto Press.

Winkelman, Michael. 1975. "Saving the American Land." *Design and Environment* 9:31.

NEWSPAPERS

Alberta Sunday *Tab.* 1978. December 3.

Camden *Courier Post.* 1977. June 13, June 16.

Department of Environmental Protection, 1976. News Release, October 4.

New Jersey Sierran. 1975. November, vol. 3, no. 7.

New York *Sun.* 1913. June 29.

New York *Times.* 1967. March 3, March 21, April 1, April 11, October 25.

New York *Times.* 1976. December 5.

New York *Times.* 1981. January 13.

DOCUMENTS

Congressional Record: House of Representatives. 1977. April 20. Statement by Congressman James J. Florio.

Congressional Record: House of Representatives. 1977. October 3. Testimony by Joan Goldstein before House Subcommittee Hearings on H.R. 6625.

Congressional Record: House of Representatives. 1977. October 12. Statement by Congressman Hughes. H.R. 6625: To establish a National Ecological Reserve.

Congressional Record: House of Representatives. 1977. October 21. Statement by Congressman Edwin B. Forsythe.

Congressional Record: House of Representatives. 1977. November 28. Testimomy of Joan Goldstein before House Subcommittee on Fish and Wildlife Hearings on H.R. 9535.

Congressional Record: Senate. 1977. November 4. S. 2306. Statement by Senator Harrison Williams.

Estimates of Land in Farms by Municipalities and County, New
 Jersey. 1971. Bulletin 840, Department of Agriculture. Prepared by Lee D. Schneider, Victor Kasper, Jr., and Dawn A.
 Derr.

H.R. 9535. 1977. Establishment of Pinelands National Wildlife
 Refuge.

Lacey Township Centennial Committee. 1971. The Hundred Years
 of Lacey Township, 1871-1971.

Letter from J. Garfield DeMarco to Commissioner David Bardin.
 September 8, 1975.

Master Plan, Bass River Township. 1975. Prepared for Bass
 River Township Planning Board, Burlington County, New Jersey,
 by John J. Holland. December.

Ocean County Historical Society. N.D. Lakewood Committee of
 the Ocean County Historical Society. Pictorial Album of Lakewood, New Jersey.

Ocean County Planning Board. 1976. Retirement Communities,
 Ocean County, New Jersey. Compiled by William W. Kuster,
 Jr. October.

Ocean County Principals' Council. 1971. Tides of Time in Ocean
 County. Cottonport, La.: Polyanthos.

Open Space for America. 1965. Prepared for the Urban Renewal
 Administration, Department of Housing and Urban Development,
 by Ann Louise Strong. Washington, D.C.

Pinelands Environmental Council. 1974. Bulltown and Friendship
 Bogs, Non-Public Lands within Wharton State Forest. Browne
 Mills, N.J.: The Conservation and Environmental Studies Center. September.

Pinelands Environmental Council. 1974. The West Plains and
 Oswego River Extensions. Browne Mills, N.J.: The Conservation and Environmental Studies Center.

Pinelands Environmental Council. 1975. Plan for the Pinelands.
 Philadelphia: Meridian Engineering.

168 / ENVIRONMENTAL DECISION MAKING

Pinelands Regional Planning Board. 1964. Future Development Plans: The New Jersey Pinelands Region. West Trenton: Herbert H. Smith Associates.

Port of New York Authority. 1961. A Report on Airport Requirements and Sites in the Metropolitan New Jersey-New York Region. May.

A Proposal for an Intercontinental Jetport and a System of General Aviation Facilities. 1967. Report of the Governor's Economic Evaluation Committee for an Intercontinental Airport for New Jersey.

S. 2306. 1977. To Establish a National System of Reserves for the Protection of Outstanding Ecological, Scenic, Historic, Cultural, and Recreational Landscapes.

Speech by former Deputy Commissioner Rocco Ricci, New Jersey Department of Environmental Protection. 1976. At the Second Annual Environmental Convention. New Brunswick, October 30.

Speech by Congressman Edwin Forsythe. 1977. Conference on the Pine Barrens. Cape May, New Jersey. February 12.

State of New Jersey. 1906. Department of State. Census Bureau. Compendium of Census, 1726-1905. New York: John L. Murphy Publishing Company.

State of New Jersey. 1957. New Jersey Agricultural Statistics, 1945-1956. New Jersey Crop Reporting Service, in cooperation with U.S. Department of Agriculture. Trenton, July.

State of New Jersey. 1971a. Assembly Bill 2096, Chapter 417, Laws of 1971.

State of New Jersey. 1971b. Department of Agriculture. Garden State Agricultural Trends. Trenton, Rural Advisory Council.

State of New Jersey. 1975a. Division of Taxation. Farmland Assessment Act of 1964. Chapter 48, Laws of 1967. Seventh Report of Data from FA-1 Forms for 1975 Tax Year. Trenton.

State of New Jersey. 1975b. New Jersey Agricultural Statistics. New Jersey Crop Reporting Service. August.

State of New Jersey. 1976. Farmland Assessment Act of 1964. Division of Taxation. September.

State of New Jersey. N.D. Department of Agriculture. Farmland Preservation.

U.S. Department of Agriculture. 1974. Economic Research Service. <u>State Programs for the Differential Assessment of Farm and Open Land</u>. Agricultural Report No. 256. Washington, D.C.

U.S. Department of the Interior. 1976. Bureau of Outdoor Recreation. <u>New Jersey Pine Barrens: Concepts for Preservation</u>.

U.S. Department of the Interior. N.D. National Park Service. <u>Pine Barrens of New Jersey</u>.

<u>Untaxing Open Space, An Evaluation of the Effectiveness of Differential Assessment of Farms and Open Space</u>. 1976. Prepared for the Council on Environmental Quality. Washington, D.C.: U.S. Government Printing Office, April.

ABOUT THE AUTHOR

JOAN GOLDSTEIN is a sociologist at Rutgers University, New Jersey. She is an appointed member of the Intergovernmental Planning Technical Working Committee on Off-Shore Oil Leasing, Outer Continental Shelf, Mid-Atlantic Region; and formerly was appointed to the governor's Pinelands Review Committee. She is now a governor's appointed member of the New Jersey Public Health Council.

Dr. Goldstein has published widely in the area of sociology and she has delivered papers internationally at conferences in Europe and Canada. Her work appears in a Canadian edited book on social impact assessment.

Dr. Goldstein holds a B.A. from the University of Iowa, an M.S. from Bank Street College, and a Ph.D. from the Graduate Center, City University of New York.